D1198380

MESSAGE OF BIBLICAL SPIRITUALITY
Editorial Director: Carolyn Osiek, RSCJ

Volume 10

The Gospel of Luke & Acts

Philip Van Linden, CM

ABOUT THE AUTHOR

Philip Van Linden, CM, was ordained a Vincentian priest in 1970. He studied for a Scripture degree in Rome, 1970-72; taught Scripture and spirituality for ten years in theologate level seminaries in Los Angeles and Chicago; and has served as a parish priest for three years in downtown Los Angeles, in a community that is predominantly Spanish-speaking.

First published in 1986 by Michael Glazier, Inc. 1935 West Fourth Street, Wilmington, Delaware, 19805. Library of Congress Catalog Card Number: 85-45558. International Standard Book Numbers: *Message of Biblical Spirituality* series: 0-89453-550-1, cloth; 0-89453-566-8, paper. LUKE/ACTS: 0-89453-560-9, cloth; 0-89453-576-5 paper. Typography by Dick Smith, Debbie Farmer, Connie Runkel. Cover design by Florence Bern. Printed in the United States of America.

TABLE OF CONTENTS

EDITOR'S PREFACE

One of the characteristics of church life today is a revived interest in spirituality. There is a growing list of resources in this area, yet the need for more is not exhausted. People are yearning for guidance in living an integrated life of faith in which belief, attitude, affections, prayer, and action form a cohesive unity which gives meaning to their lives.

The biblical tradition is a rich resource for the variety of ways in which people have heard God's call to live a life of faith and fidelity. In each of the biblical books we have a witness to the initiative of God in human history and to the attempts of people not so different from ourselves to respond to the revelation of God's love and care.

The fifteen volumes in the *Message of Biblical Spirituality* series aim to provide ready access to the treasury of biblical faith. Modern social science has made us aware of how the particular way in which one views reality conditions the ways in which one will interpret experience and life itself. Each volume in this series is an attempt to retell and interpret the biblical story from within the faith perspective that originally formed it. Each seeks to portray what it is like to see God, the world, and oneself from a particular point of view and to search for ways to respond faithfully to that vision. We who are citizens of our twentieth century world cannot be people of the ancient biblical world, but we can grow closer to their experience and their faith and thus closer to God, through the living Word of God which is the Bible.

The series includes an international group of authors representing England, Ireland, Canada, and the United States, but whose life experience has included first-hand knowledge of many other countries. All are proven scholars and committed believers whose faith is as important to them as their scholarship. Each acts as interpreter of one part of the biblical tradition in order to enable its spiritual vitality to be passed on to others. It is our hope that through their labor the reader will be able to enter more deeply into the life of faith, hope, and love through a fuller understanding of and appreciation for the biblical Word as handed down to us by God's faithful witnesses, the biblical authors themselves.

Carolyn Osiek, RSCJ
Associate Professor of New Testament Studies
Catholic Theological Union, Chicago

ACKNOWLEDGEMENTS

This spiritual journey with Luke's Jesus has been a joyfilled and energizing experience for me. What began as a rather auspicious challenge ("How can I expect to write this book and also carry on my parish ministry responsibly?") gradually came to be a "labor of love." I am almost sorry to see it come to an end.

I have learned so much. I have discovered anew God's love for me and for his people. I have come to appreciate his word and Luke's literary genius as never before. I have learned how to serve God's people a little better, motivated by the "Lucan spirit." I have also learned how to let them love me and teach me the ways of the Lord.

As a priest of the community of St. Vincent de Paul, I had long desired to be among the poor and "to leave God for God," that is, even to leave prayer in order to respond to the cry of the poor. However, during this year of writing, I found myself applying this saying of Vincent to my life in a new way. For me, it came to mean: "Phil, do not be afraid to leave the people in order to write." I believe that this time, spent with Jesus and Luke, has been a concrete way for me to "bring glad tidings to the poor" and to "announce a year of favor to the Lord" (Lk 4:18f.). I hope that those who read this book will agree that it was time and effort well-spent on behalf of the Body of Christ.

As I conclude this work on the spiritual vision of Luke-Acts, I want to "offer praise to you, Father, Lord of heaven and earth. For what you have hidden from the learned and the clever you have revealed to the merest children" (Lk 10:21). I also express my deep gratitude to my family and friends, to my Vincentian brothers and other coworkers in the Lord's vineyard, for all their love and support. Finally, I thank the faithfilled parishioners and children of St. Vincent de Paul parish, in South Central Los Angeles, for teaching me to reverence them and myself, as coequal brothers and sisters in Jesus Christ. *It is he who said it.* "How much more important each one of you is than the birds of the air! Your Father knows all that you need. Seek out his kingship over you, and the rest will follow in turn. Wherever your treasure is, there your heart will also be" (Lk 12:24, 30, & 34). *It is the people in my life who have lived it*!

The Christian journey goes on. Let us travel it together. Thanks be to God!

September 27, 1985
Feast of St. Vincent
Los Angeles, California

INTRODUCTION

Like St. Luke, who drew together many strains of Christian tradition about Jesus for the sake of his first century readers and their needs, I, too, found myself organizing this treatment of the spirituality of Luke's writings around my perception of the needs of twentieth century Christians. For us, as for Luke's first readers, *the spiritual life is much like a journey.* That is why Part One of this book concerns the spiritual journey with Jesus and serves as the framework for all that follows. On such a journey, it is vital that companions of Jesus look to their prayer union with him as the source of what they do as Christians. Consequently, Part Two concentrates on *discerning God's will in one's life through prayer,* the indispensable means of being in tune with God's Spirit. However, any spirituality that is worthy of the name "Christian" must flow into concrete action. The saying, "by their fruits you will know them," is as true for Luke's readers today as it was in the first Christian century. Therefore, Part Three of this books deals with Lucan "themes for the journey," and it calls for specific *Christian responses in the day-to-day lives* of its readers. The fact that the first theme treated in Part Three concerns "The Poor And The

Rich" might betray a personal bias, since I am a Vincentian priest. Like many religious communities, ours is primarily dedicated to the evangelization of the poor. However, even with such a prejudice taken into account, I believe that the choice and ordering of themes in this book is pretty much in line with Luke's own preferences, since Luke himself chose to have Jesus begin his earthly ministry with the words: "The Spirit of the Lord is upon me . . . He has sent me to bring glad tidings to the poor" (4:18). In Part Four there is a "break in the flow" of these Lucan themes. This is meant to be similar to the pause which Luke provided for his readers as he moved from his gospel to the Acts of the Apostles. In that pause, his audience could sit back and marvel at his gospel presentation of Jesus prior to embarking on the exciting journey with the early church in Acts. The "interlude for marvelling" in this book is intended to deepen its readers' appreciation for *Luke as literary genius.* More specifically, Part Four highlights Luke as an author who communicates as forcefully through the literary structure of his gospel as through the themes it emphasizes. The final section, Part Five, takes up *more Lucan themes,* and it ends with "Joy: The Final Chapter." This seemed to me to be an appropriate way to conclude this study of Lucan spirituality, for two reasons. First, only a life imbued with true Christian joy can truly be called Lucan. Secondly, it is with a great deal of personal joy that I present my readers with the fruit of my own involvement with Luke on his *and our* spiritual journey with Jesus.

Part I

The Spiritual Life as a Journey

1

THE CHRISTIAN LIFE AS A SPIRITUAL JOURNEY

A pilgrim is a person "on the way." A spiritual pilgrim is anyone who is trying "to get somewhere with God." Throughout the centuries, spiritual writers of the Judeo-Christian tradition have thus tried to describe their experience of life with God in the imagery and language of *journey*. God's people are characterized as "a people on pilgrimage." The Gospel of Luke and his Acts of the Apostles provide one of the richest sources for such a vision of the Christian life. Upon encountering God's word according to Luke, Christians will find themselves invited to accompany the Lord of their life on an exciting spiritual journey, one that involves them at the very core of their being, as members of a pilgrim people.

This guide to Luke's writings begins, therefore, with a brief description of Christian spirituality in terms of one's personal journey with God. It will then attempt to place Luke in the context of his times and the traditions he received. What emerges from this look at Luke and his times is the conclusion that Luke's gospel and Acts are an indispensable link between the profound experience of God's Hebrew people "on the way" and the Christian church which Luke addresses, first, in the age of transition at the end of the first Christian century, and now, as God's pilgrim people "still on the way," until journey's end.

The Journey with God

Life with God is not a static moment in time. Rather, it is a process of persons growing in relationship with a person, who is their Lord. On the way, there are "ups and downs," times for rest and reflection, times of crisis and upheaval, and times of deep joy. The word of God provides a certain direction for the pilgrimage, but Christian pilgrims readily sense the need for special guidance and assistance at times from fellow travelers. They look to people with similar or even more experience with God "on the way." Primarily, they believe that their risen Lord is with them through the guiding inspiration of the Holy Spirit. They want an ever deeper relationship with him in prayer. The journey is life long, so there are things to take along. Necessary changes and adaptations have to be made. As the travellers grow older and wiser in the way of Christian pilgrims, it becomes even clearer that they do not travel alone, that they are not the first to go this way and that they will not be the last. In fact, the wisest pilgrims gradually realize that, even when their personal journeys have ended, there will still be a time of waiting, until all of God's children have completed their pilgrimage. They know this from their experience of life and death and hope. They understand what Paul says to the church at Rome.

> Yes, we know that all creation groans and is in agony even until now. Not only that, but we ourselves, although we have the Spirit as first fruits, groan inwardly while we await the redemption of our bodies. (Romans 8:23).

They believe that the goal of their individual journeys is the face to face, eternal union of God and all his people. On that day, when "Christ, the first fruits, and all those who belong to him come to life again," and when "God is all in all," the Christian journey, a family affair, will truly come to its end (1 Cor 15:22, 28).

Our Spiritual Journey: Rooted in Hebrew Scripture

The "journey mode" of expressing the way God and his people have been together is not original with Luke. It is firmly rooted in the Hebrew scriptures. Abraham, "our father in the faith," has been traditionally described in vivid terms as a pilgrim, led by God from Ur at seventy-five years of age (Gen 12:4).

> My father (Abraham) was a wandering Aramean who went down to Egypt with a small household and *lived there as an alien*. But then he became a nation, great, strong, and numerous. When the Egyptians maltreated us, God *brought us out* of Egypt. *And bringing us* to this country, he gave us this land, flowing with milk and honey. (Dt 26:5-9).

Those who recorded this core Exodus event expressed the people's experience of God as a way, a journey, a moving experience of their God. Even the term they used for the journey, *derek* in Hebrew, is particularly expressive. From the beginning this word had a two-fold meaning. The first level of meaning was simply "a way, a path, a road on which one travels to a destination." But the term also meant "a way of living," that is, the way of living according to God's law: "Keep the commandments of the Lord, your God by *walking in his ways* and fearing him" (Dt 8:6).

God was always intimately involved with his people on their journey as "the main character of the drama." He was their guiding leader and force on the way. "Remember this day on which you came out of Egypt, that place of slavery. It was with a strong right hand that the Lord brought you away" (Exodus 13:3). Even after the deliverance from Egypt, God led his people into the desert, where they were tested "in the ways of the Lord."

> Remember how for forty years now, *the Lord, your God, has directed all your journeying* in the desert, so as to test you by affliction and to find out whether or not it was your intention to keep his commandments. (Dt 8:2).

In the desert, the people balked at God's ways and even wanted to go back to Egypt, on their own: "Why is the Lord bringing us into this land only to have us fall by the sword? Would it not be better for us to return to Egypt?" (Numbers 14:3).

Through the mediation of Moses, the people were invited to enter a covenant with God in the desert. It was there, at Mount Horeb, that a people was formed for the final leg of the journey, the entrance into the promised land.

However, the Hebrew people's journey did not end once they had arrived in the promised land. The prophets took up the Exodus theme and interpreted the people's continuing experience of God by urging them to live on "according to his way."

> In speaking to your fathers, *on the day I brought them out* of Egypt, I gave them no command concerning sacrifices or holocausts. This is rather what I commanded them: listen to my voice. Then I will be your God and you shall be my people. *Walk in the ways* I command you, so that you may prosper. (Jer 7:22f).

The people's journey with God from Ur, out of Egypt, through the desert, and into the promised land, had now become "the way of living there" with their God.

The Journey with God: A Corporate Affair of Unfinished Business

Key to the Hebrew people's spiritual experience of God is the unfolding understanding of themselves as a special *people.* It was an individual, Abram, whom God first called to travel with and for him: "Go forth from the land of your kinsfolk and from your father's house to a land I will show you" (Gen 12:1). Along the way, as Abram continued to *walk blamelessly in God's presence,* the Lord appeared to him and said:

> My covenant with you is this: you are to become the father of a host of nations. No longer shall you be called Abram (literally, the father is exalted); your name shall be called Abraham, for I am making you 'the father of a host of nations'. (Gen 17:4-5).

The promises God made to his special people were not meant for Abram alone, nor for his own limited family. They were meant for his entire people of the covenant. Indeed, his promises would be fulfilled for all his people. The small band of people God delivered from Egypt, under Moses' leadership, became his own people "on the way," in the desert part of their journey with him. This happened after much testing of their fidelity to "God's ways." They entered the promised land as a people, and to this day, are aware of the reality that their journey continues as a *corporate journey*.

A final look at the Hebrew people's journey experience with their God focuses on the prophet Isaiah's message to a people enslaved once again, this time in Babylon.

> Comfort, give comfort to my people, says your God. Speak tenderly to Jerusalem, and proclaim to her that her service is at an end, her guilt is expiated. A voice cries out: In the desert *prepare the way of the Lord*! Make straight in the wasteland *a highway* for our God! (Is 40:1-3).

And to make sure that his forgiven and redeemed people would realize the life-long nature of his relationship with them, God further proclaims through Isaiah:

> Remember not the events of the past, the things of long ago consider not. See, I am doing something new! Now it springs forth, do you not perceive it? In the desert *I make a way*, in the wasteland, rivers. Wild beasts honor me, jackals and ostriches, for I put water in the desert and rivers in the wasteland for my chosen people to drink, the people I formed for myself, that they might announce my praise. (Is 43:18-22).

Christian Spirituality: Jesus Is the Way

The earliest written record of first generation Christianity comes from the letters of Paul. This Christianity, formed in the saving event of Jesus' death and resurrection, was intimately bound to Judaism. The "pillars of the church" (Peter, James, and John) resided and judged from Jerusalem (Gal 2:1-10). The earliest Christian mission was properly to Jesus' own people, the Jews. From his letters, it is clear that Paul continually had to defend his work among the Gentiles.

Then came 70 A.D. and the destruction of Jerusalem by the Romans. At the same time that the last leaders of first generation Christianity were dying for their faith, as did Stephen, Peter, and Paul, the tragedy of Roman occupation of their "mother city" stunned the whole Jewish community, of which Christian Jews were a part. All Jews were dispersed by the Romans. All were held suspect as revolutionaries by the Roman controllers of the Mid-east. No longer was it necessary for Paul to "go up to Jerusalem" to confer with the authoritative leaders of the Christian community (Gal 2:1). A Jewish Jerusalem existed no more! No longer did "the pagan mission" have to be justified, because second generation Christianity would survive the storm of the fall of Jerusalem by becoming more and more independent from Judaism. And it survived as a community made up of *both* Jewish and Gentile Christians. The death and resurrection of Jesus had formed a new people for God. The fall the Jerusalem had given it a new identity.

It was in this "age of transition" that Luke lived and wrote. Along with his own experience of Jesus and the Christian life, Luke looked back to draw together oral and written traditions about his risen Lord for the Gentile and Jewish community that adhered to Christ. As he reflected on his sources for Jesus' life, which he had at his disposal (e.g., the gospel of Mark and the legacy of Paul's letters), Luke gradually saw God's saving history unfold in a bright new light. The journey had taken a new turn in crisis times. The people formed by God in the desert was created anew on the cross and was set on a new course by the events of 70 A.D. It was Luke who set out to transmit this "good news" in his gospel and Acts.

2

THE JOURNEY WITH JESUS

Luke has long been recognized by scripture scholars as the most artistic and skilled writer of the four evangelists. He knows how to use the finest Greek and turn the finest phrase. He has composed and passed on the most memorable gospel stories. What scholars have also pointed out is the marvelous way Luke has joined the imagery and vocabulary of "journey" with a carefully structured pattern of composition, thereby presenting his readers with a two-volume work that is a flowing, unified, cohesive whole. To that "journey vocabulary" and "journey structure" we now turn, in order to walk even more closely with Jesus.

Mary and John Prepare Jesus' Way

As Abraham, Moses, and the prophets prepared God's people and guided them on their journey with God, so also did

Mary and John the Baptist prepare the way for the church's walk with Jesus. *Mary,* the trusting servant of the Lord, was constantly "on the move." According to Luke, she journeyed through the hill country of Judea to bring the good news of Jesus' birth to John's mother, Elizabeth (1:39-56). After going to Bethlehem, where she gave birth to her own son (2:4-7), she and Joseph went up to Jerusalem to present him to the Lord (2:22ff.). She would also pilgrimage to Jerusalem with her twelve year old son for his first passover celebration (2:41), only to learn that he had to "be about his father's business there" (2:49). In time, after journeying with Jesus a final time (was she not among "the women who had come with him from Galilee" to be there at his death? 23:55), she would grasp more fully what he had said as a child of twelve. Mary was a pilgrim woman, journeying with Jesus from the womb until his death, and beyond. *John the Baptist,* for his part, became the herald promised by Isaiah. He was the one who finally made ready the way of the Lord and cleared him a straight path, "by proclaiming a baptism of repentance which led to the forgiveness of sin" (3:3f.; Isaiah 40:3ff.). John's role, according to his father, Zechariah, was to go before the Lord, "to prepare paths for him, so that he could visit his people in mercy and guide their feet into the way of peace" (1:76-79).

Jesus' Own Journey

While all four of the gospel writers construct their narratives around Jesus' journey to his passion and death in Jerusalem, none does so in such a careful, plotted way as Luke. Luke adopts the imagery and language of the Exodus experience to make it obvious to his readers that Jesus' way is the *new Exodus.* Like the people who wandered in the desert for forty years, Luke's Jesus, "full of the Holy Spirit, returned from the Jordan and was conducted by the Spirit into the desert for forty days, where he was tempted by the devil" (4:1). Once he had proven to be a faithful son, rejecting the desert temptations of the devil, "he returned in the power of the Spirit to Galilee," where his mission would begin. Throughout Jesus' mission of healing and preaching, Luke strains to keep his readers aware of Jesus' role as *the one going before them,* bringing them out of slavery as his Father brought his people out of Egypt long before. During the transfiguration scene, for example, only Luke has Moses and Elijah speak "of Jesus' *passage,* which he was about to fulfill in Jerusalem" (9:31; the Greek word for *passage* which Luke uses is *exodus*). Later, as the time was approaching when Jesus would decide to face what was in store for him, Luke chooses to say it this way: "He firmly resolved to proceed toward Jerusalem, and he sent messengers on ahead of him. These entered a Samaritan town to prepare for his *passing through,* but the Samaritans would not welcome him because he was *on his way* to Jerusalem" (9:51-53). Now, Samaritans were hostile to anyone who was journeying to Jerusalem, for there was a mutual dislike between Samaritans and Judean Jews. This could explain the language used in this passage in a simple way. However, the "journey motif" of Luke is so strong in his gospel that one can be fairly sure that he intended to keep his readers on Jesus' Exodus route. This is crystal clear in the pivotal section in chapter 13, where Jesus is warned by the Pharisees: "Go on your way! Leave this place! Herod is trying to kill you!" (v.31). And Jesus responded:

> Go tell that fox, today and tomorrow I cast out devils and perform cures, and on the third day my purpose is accomplished. For all that, I must *proceed on course* today, tomorrow, and the day after, since no prophet can be allowed to die anywhere except in Jerusalem. (13:31-33).

Finally, Luke signals the end of Jesus' earthly pilgrimage with the stark phrase: "Having spoken thus, he *went ahead with his ascent* to Jerusalem" (19:28).

Luke uses a variety of Greek terms to describe Jesus' journey as a way, a road, a course, an ascent, etc. Still, his gospel and Acts carry over the basic two-fold meaning of the single Hebrew word used for journey, *derek*: it is the path on which one journeys, both literally and figuratively. Consequently, Christians who want to put on a Lucan spirituality will follow Jesus as pilgrim travellers on their earthly journey, imitating his "way of living according to God's design." They will be challenged to follow Luke's Jesus *up the road*, taking nothing for the journey, and saluting no one on the way, if that would hinder their progress (9:3, 57, & 10:4). They will listen to him as the Emmaus disciples did when he talks with them on the road, through dialogue with his living word (24:32). They will follow "the Dayspring, who shines on those who sit in darkness and the shadow of death, and guides their feet into the way of peace" (1:79).

The Church's Journey in Acts: The New Way

Even before the followers of Jesus were first called "Christians" (at Antioch; see Acts 11:26), their lifestyle had come to be known as "the way" (Acts 9:2; see also 18:25-26). As Jesus' way had *led up to* Jerusalem and the saving events there, the "new way" was destined to *spread out from* Jerusalem *to the ends of the earth* (24:47 and Acts 1:8). To be a member of the new way did not mean a static acceptance of Jesus' teachings. It meant a dynamic following in Jesus' footsteps and an opening up of the church's horizons to all peoples. Consequently, guided by the Spirit of their risen Lord, Peter, Paul, and the whole early church quickly progressed along on its way, outward bound, to the Gentiles.

As Peter and his companions were "travelling along and approaching Caesarea, he went up on the roof terrace to pray" (Acts 10:9). The ensuing vision Peter received from the Spirit, as well as his encounter with Cornelius, brought the good news of Jesus' way to the Gentiles: " 'What can stop these people (the non-Jews of Cornelius' household), who have received the Holy Spirit, even as we (Jews) have, from being baptized with water?' So Peter gave orders that they be baptized in the name of Jesus Christ" (Acts 10:47f.).

Paul's mission to the Gentiles began, significantly enough, on a road, the road to Damascus. Luke has Barnabas describe it in this way: "He explained to them how *on his journey* Saul had seen the Lord, who had conversed with him, and how Saul had been speaking out fearlessly in the name of Jesus at Damascus" (Acts 9:27f.). Through their encounters with the Spirit and the risen Lord, Peter and Paul's journeys became Christ's continuing journey with his people. Indeed, Paul's preaching of the new way to the Gentiles would parallel, in many ways, Jesus' mission to his own people. As Jesus met with much opposition on his journey to Jerusalem, so would Paul's preaching cause much controversy. "In their obstinacy, some Jewish and Greek Ephesians would not believe, but chose to speak ill of *the new way* in the presence of the assembly" (Acts 19:9). "Serious disturbances broke out concerning *the new way*" when Paul was found persuading great numbers of people to change their religion at Ephesus (Acts 19:23-26). Just as Jesus chose his "Twelve" to join him on his journey, Paul soon drew to himself co-ministers, like Priscilla and Aquila, who learned how to catechize Jews and Greeks alike in the new way. When Paul left them for Syria, Apollos, "an authority on scripture and one instructed in *the new way*," (18:24f.) came to join them in Ephesus. They immediately took him home "to explain *God's new way* in greater detail" (18:26). Through controversy and cooperation, Jesus' message wound its way through the Mid-east toward Rome. It was done, says Luke, in imitation of Jesus, even unto the end of the journey. Thus Paul can sum up his entire ministry in this way:

> With Jews and Greeks alike I insisted solemnly on repentance before God and on faith in our Lord Jesus. But now, as you see, I am *on my way to Jerusalem*, compelled by the Spirit and not knowing what will happen to me there — except that the Holy Spirit has been warning me from city to city that chains and hardships await me. I put no value on my life, if only I *can finish my course* and complete the service to which I have been assigned by the Lord Jesus, bearing witness to the gospel of God's grace. (Acts 20:21-24).

Paul's course had become Jesus' course, the way of the Spirit. Paul's ministry ended in Jerusalem, as Jesus' had. He was tried there by Roman officials, just like Jesus. He would eventually die as Jesus did, witnessing to God's good news. However, the Acts of the Apostles leaves him, and Luke's readers, carrying on the unfinished business of Jesus, the Spirit, and the church, in Rome.

> 'Now you must realize that this salvation of God has been transmitted to Gentiles — who will heed it!' And for two full years Paul stayed on in his rented lodgings, welcoming all who came to him. With full assurance, and without any hindrance whatever, he preached the reign of God and taught about the Lord Jesus Christ. (Acts 28:28-31).

The journey of the early church, as described by Luke, thus ends on an unfinished note. The journey continues in the life of the church-in-time, in the twentieth century, as well as in Luke's first century community of faith. It is the new way of Jesus in the new day, today!

The Journey Structure of Luke-Acts

All of the *journey terminology* of Luke-Acts gives more than sufficient direction to twentieth century Christians in search of a dynamic and enlivening relationship with Jesus. Luke, however, has gone to even further lengths to involve his readers on their walk with their Lord. He has carefully woven his journey terminology into an overall *journey literary structure,* which can be seen "in a glance" in the following diagram:

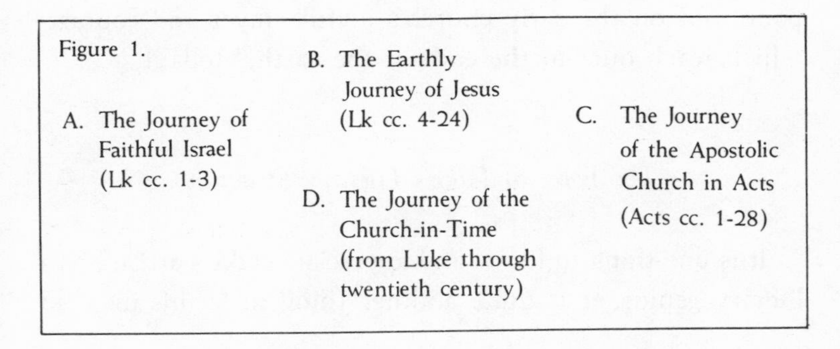

According to Figure 1, one can stand with Luke's first audience, in 80 A.D., in order to look back to "the center of time," namely, Jesus' earthly Journey B. From its perspective of Journey D, the church takes Jesus as its focus and model for its own pilgrim way to God. Christians do not look back fifty years (or nineteen hundred and fifty years) only to remember the "history" of Jesus. They look back with the eyes of Luke, in order to base their Christian life-project on Jesus' own lived-out faith in God. Thanks to Luke's literary genius, they also have vivid models of what a living Christian community is like in those who preceded Jesus (Journey A.) and in those who first followed him (Journey C). Journey A features Mary, John the Baptist, Zechariah, Simeon, and Anna, who prepared the way for Jesus by their faithful adherence to the God of Israel. Journey C features Peter, Paul, and all the memcrable characters of the primitive Christian family, who patterned their mission on Jesus' life and gave themselves over to the guidance of the Holy Spirit. As faithful Israel *looked forward* to Jesus, and as the faithful church in Acts *looked back* to him for direction, so does the church of Luke look to all three "journeys" for inspired guidance. In this way, it can learn how to pattern its day-to-day spirituality on God's tender mercy toward his beloved people, on Jesus' passionate love of the poor, and on the early church's joyful prayer and courage, which reach out "to the ends of the earth," today!

The Force of Luke's Literary Structure

It is one thing to know and appreciate Luke's artistry as a literary genius. It is quite another thing to let his inspired two-volume masterpiece be a source of energy for Christian living. To assist Luke's readers to experience the force of his "journey structure," three "side trips" are presented in the pages that follow: 1) an example of the life-giving parallelism found in Luke and Acts; 2) an example of positive character transformation that occurs from the gospel to the Acts; 3) a key to finishing Luke's "unfinished business." Finally, this chapter will conclude with a practical suggestion for walking with Jesus in prayer.

Jesus and the Church Give Life: Then and Now

Early in Jesus' ministry (see Lk 8:40-56), a man named Jairus came to him, begging that he accompany him to his home where his only daughter was dying. Jesus started out with Jairus, pressing his way through the crowds around him. On the way, some people informed Jairus that his daughter was already dead. Jesus heard this and said: "Fear is useless; what is needed is trust and her life will be spared." And they pressed on. Upon arrival there, Jesus permitted no one but the girl's parents and Peter, James, and John to enter. Within earshot of the weeping crowd of mourners outside, Jesus took her by the hand and said: "Get up, child." The breath of life returned to her, and she immediately got up. Then Jesus asked her parents to give her something to eat, which, for Luke's readers, was as much a "proof" that the girl was really alive, as it was a sign of Jesus' concern that she might be hungry.

The gospels of Matthew and Mark also record this event, with more or less the same careful detail and drama (see Mt 9:18-26 and Mk 5:21-43). Both of them want to convey the same message, namely, that Jesus is the source of life for those who trust in him. However, Luke "doubles the impact" of this miracle story, not by changes he makes in recounting it, but by presenting a parallel account in his Journey C, the journey of the church. By so doing, Luke says that "even after Jesus is no longer walking with his people on this earth, as Jesus of Nazareth, his life-giving power is still available for those who trust." Or so it would seem, when (in Acts 9:32-43) Peter "was making various journeys and went, among other places, to God's holy people living in Lydda." There, in almost exact parallel with the Jesus and Jairus story of the gospel, some people came to Peter, requesting that he go to the house of Tabitha, a woman convert who had just died. Upon arrival at the house, Peter first made all her friends stay outside. Then he said, just as Jesus had, "Tabitha, stand up." She opened her eyes, then looked at Peter, and sat up. He gave her his hand, helped her up, and the next thing he did was call in the believers and her widow friends to show them that she was alive!

When we notice the many parallels in these two accounts from Luke 8 and Acts 9, the power of the gospel story is reinforced in the continuing story of the church. Namely, in Jesus people have life! Fear is useless, even in the face of death! Most importantly, those who journey as Jesus did before them, can give life to others! The ongoing journey of Christians is meant to be a life-giving journey. And however that life is given, whether it is the very breath of life being restored to a dying person by a dedicated surgeon, or whether it is the consoling and uplifting embrace for those who have just lost a loved one in death, the church can make present today the life that is rooted in trusting the Lord.

From the Gospel to the Acts: Faith Development

When one travels all the way through Luke's gospel and Acts, there emerge some inspiring cases of faith development. Paul's dramatic conversion from sinner to saint is a marvelous example of God's transforming grace (see Acts 7:54-8:3 & 9:1-22). But the transformation of Peter is more complex, more gradual, and more revealing of the spiritual insight of Luke. A brief look at two moments in Peter's life, one in the gospel and the other in the Acts, will suffice to bring out the dynamism of Luke's two-volume composition.

One would expect that the first person whom Jesus chose to be his intimate companion, would, indeed, prove faithful to the end. The church knows better from all four gospels, which preserve the account of Peter's denial of Jesus in the courtyard (in Luke, 22:54-62). He failed to live up to his calling to follow Jesus. Yet, through Luke's presentation of the Acts, Christians have also come to know how Peter rebounded in the Spirit, to become the most courageous proclaimer of the gospel, in the face of all odds (see Acts cc. 2-5). Peter's valor and preaching would eventually challenge both Jew and Gentile to the hope and truth of Jesus' divine sonship (Acts cc. 9-11). More significantly, by showing Peter's gradual growth in faith over his two-volume work, Luke is able to give hope to all his readers, no matter at what stage of faith development they find themselves.

Jesus' Unfinished Business: It's Up to the Church

It has long been noted that Luke's Acts of the Apostles

(Journey C) takes up where his gospel (Journeys A and B) ends. It seems that his original unified work was "broken in two" during the second Christian century formation of the new testament "canon" (the approved collection of inspired writings). At that time, the four gospels were drawn together as a unit, as were the letters of Paul. Luke's book of Acts was left to "fit in between" the gospel of John and Paul's letter to the Romans. Nonetheless, even a casual reading of the ending of Luke's gospel and the beginning of his Acts, reveals that the gospel is an open-ended book, finding some closure and much fulfillment in the Spirit-life of the church. The remarkable part of it is, however, that Luke's Acts of the Apostles is also "a gospel waiting to be completed." With Paul preaching God's reign "with full assurance" (Acts 28:31), Luke leaves his readers with the definite impression that it is up to them to complete the journey begun in Mary, Jesus, and the early church. The open-ended nature of Luke's literary masterpiece points to the unfinished business of the Christian journey. It is up to the twentieth century church to let the Spirit guide it on its part of the way (Journey D).

Luke has truly blessed the church with the opportunity to interact with the many holy and human characters of his inspired drama. Those who have preceded today's disciples of Jesus now wait for them at journey's end. The memorable Lucan characters of the gospel and Acts have all completed their pilgrimage. So have many others, who have walked with Jesus since that first Christian century. All those who have finished their course of Christian discipleship on earth, now invite the church to follow the light, the Spirit of God, guiding it into the way of peace. They also eagerly await the day when all the pilgrims of Journeys A, B, C, and D, will witness the coming of the Son of Man "on a cloud, with great power and glory" (21:27). On that day, the Christian journey will be no more. The final chapter of Luke's gospel will be completed. All of God's people will be home with him.

A Practical Suggestion for Putting on Luke's "Journey Spirituality"

In the preceding pages, it has become clear that Luke wants his readers to be involved in a life-long process of pilgrimage and love with Jesus. To conclude this section on Luke's journey with Jesus, a simple recommendation is presented here for "putting on Christ" as a co-traveller with Luke.

When Luke and other spiritual writers encourage their readers to join Jesus "on his journey," it is their primary intention to promote a whole way of life with Jesus, a complete mode of radical Christian living. However, the "first level" meaning of the term "way," namely, "a roadway, a pathway, a walkway," suggests a concrete, literal walk with Jesus. It has already been noted that Luke himself inspires the suggestion that follows, when he has Jesus "walk along with his two disciples" on the road to Emmaus (24:15). So, let Luke's readers take a slow walk with Jesus.

A Slow Walk with Jesus

In these modern times of rapid jet travel and "fast lane" pace on freeways and in personal lives, to choose to pray by walking very slowly can be a source of blessing and a powerful means of personal encounter with Jesus. Such a walk goes so much against the grain and the normal "hurry around" approach to daily life, that the person praying is almost lifted into another realm of being. Walking two or three times more slowly than usual might look strange. It will also feel strange, at first. Walking that slowly gets one no place. It can, however, so slow down the pace of life that one might allow a movement within to occur, a shift from distress about *many* things to openness to the *one* thing God wants: complete presence with himself!

Once the slow walk with Jesus has calmed the body, the mind and the heart can more easily be freed from too much thinking. The person can more readily say: "Lord, let *me* experience what *you* want in this prayer." Perhaps, God's desire will be to lead his beloved on a peaceful review of the many blessings and gifts he has given the person this day, during the past week, or even over the course of the person's whole life: blessings like good weather or good health or good friends; gifts like a breathtaking sunrise, a refreshing rainfall, or a delicate butterfly, resting on a flower before continuing on its way. Maybe the praying person will be inspired by God to recall and savor a scene from the gospels in which Jesus draws some hurting man or woman to himself in healing, pardon, or enlightening dialogue. Or perhaps one of the prophets will be heard crying out in the deep recesses of one's being, as if God were asking this one, special child of his to enter into intimate dialogue with himself.

> I will be the God of all the tribes of Israel, and they shall be my people. The people that escaped the sword have found favor in the desert. As Israel comes forward to be given his rest, the Lord appears to him from afar: '*With age-old love I have loved you;*

> so I have kept my mercy toward you. Again I will restore you, and you shall be rebuilt, O virgin Israel. (Jer 31:1-4a).
>
> Behold, I will bring back my people from the land of the north; I will gather them from the ends of the world, with the blind and the lame in their midst, the mothers and those with child; they shall return as an immense throng. They departed in tears, but I will console them and guide them; I will lead them to brooks of water, on a level road, so that none shall stumble. *For I am a father to Israel.* Ephraim is my first-born (Jer 31:8f.)
>
> *I hear, I hear Ephraim* pleading: 'You chastised me, and I am chastened; I was an untamed calf. If you allow me, I will return, for you are the Lord, my God. I turn in repentance: I have come to myself, I strike my breast: I blush with shame, I bear the disgrace of my youth.'
>
> Is Ephraim not my favored child, the son in whom I delight? Often as I threaten him, I still remember him with favor. *My heart stirs for him,* I *must* show him mercy, says the Lord. (Jer 31:18-20).

A very slow walk with the Lord can, indeed, change a person's whole perspective on life. Luke wants his readers today to be like Ephraim of old, to return to their merciful Father. He wants them to be like the Emmaus disciples, who invited their Lord to walk along with them, who begged him to stay with them, and who "let their hearts burn as he talked with them *on the road*" (24:15, 29 & 32).

3

LUKE'S JESUS: A COMPANION, POWERFUL AND SENSITIVE

To know Jesus intimately, as *the* companion on the spiritual journey, is the single most important experience of a Christian's life. It is the *sine qua non,* the *without which* the church cannot be Christian. Through prayer, life experience, and the practice of loving others, God's people grow in the intimate knowledge and experience of Jesus. They also have at their disposal a special gift that God has chosen to reveal his son to them, the Christian scriptures. All four of the inspired gospel writers had come to know and love their risen Lord as members of the primitive Christian community. In their gospel narratives, each passes on the sacred traditions he has received, but each gospel is also stamped with the special seal of each evangelist's own particular relationship with God and Jesus. Matthew, Mark, Luke, and John all present Jesus as the powerful miracle worker and charismatic teacher, who died and rose to form a people dedicated to God. As Christians today attempt to become more united with God and Jesus, it is most helpful to examine each individual evangelist's portrait of Jesus, and thus come to know him "from all sides," that is, from four inspired points of view. Several key Lucan passages will bring out the special Jesus they will meet in the pages of Luke's portrait of their companion "on the way."

A Call to "Move on" with Dignity

Jesus' opening sermon in Luke's gospel is a call of freedom and glad tidings for the poor and oppressed (4:18-21). His first miracles exhilarate the crowds who "go in search of him and try to keep him from leaving them" (4:42). Just as those "who were there" wanted Jesus to stay with them, Luke's readers are drawn to this initial picture of their mighty Lord, and they, too, might be inclined to "keep him from leaving them." But Luke's Jesus has to move on: "To other towns I must announce the good news of the reign of God, because that is why I was sent" (4:43). Therefore, says Luke, "If you want to know Jesus more personally, you must journey with him, where *he* leads. Come along. I will show you God's son."

In both the Matthean and Marcan accounts of Jesus' first days of active ministry, Jesus selects his coworkers immediately after his desert temptation experience (Mt 4:18ff., Mk 1:16ff.). That is, *before* he embarks on his healing mission, Jesus chooses his companions to go with him. Not so in Luke's version. Luke reverses this "order of events" and has Jesus call the first disciples *after* he has already begun his preaching and healing (i.e., in 5:1-11). It is as if Luke is saying to his readers: "You already know me. You have already had enough proof of my love and care for you. You like what you see. Now, I want you to realize that I know you as you are. And I want you to come with me where I go, as my cotravellers and coworkers." The way Luke does this, in 5:1-11, touches the deepest chords of the human spirit in all who wish to respond to his invitation.

> As he stood by the Lake of Gennesaret, and the crowd pressed in on him to hear the word of God, he saw two boats moored by the side of the lake; the fishermen had embarked and were washing their nets. He got into one of the boats, Simon's, and asked him to pull out a short distance from the shore . . . From there he continued to teach the crowds . . . He then said to Simon, 'Put out into deep water and lower your nets for the catch.' (vv.1-5)

Although they had not caught a thing all night long, they caught so many fish "that their nets were at the breaking point" (v.6). So startled were they all at the sight of this that Peter fell at the knees of Jesus, saying: "Leave me, Lord. I am a sinful man" (v.8).

By this vivid picture of Peter at the knees of Jesus, in his *first* encounter with him, Luke summons forth one of the most profound sentiments and common responses of humanity before God: "You are God. I am a sinner. I am not worthy even to be near you." But Luke's Jesus then lifts up Simon Peter, along with all his disciples, with the consoling and inviting words: "Do not be afraid. From now on you will be catching, not fish, but great numbers of others for the kingdom of God" (v.10). In other words, the basic sketch of Luke's portrait of Jesus consists in welcoming and accepting strokes: "I accept you as you are. I want you to come with me. I invite you to use your talents, your vocation, and your personality, as I transform them into mine. Do not be afraid. I need you as much as you need me."

Luke wants to impress his readers, from the very start, that Jesus welcomes them, no matter what their feelings of unworthiness might be. They are reassured of their dignity, in spite of their sinfulness, in this first encounter of Jesus and Peter. "Do not be afraid. Come with me." This encouraging picture of Jesus, the welcoming companion, is seen again in early pages of Luke's Acts of the Apostles. In fact, the scene in Acts 3:2-8 is like an instant replay of Luke 5:1-11. Only one thing really differs. In the Acts, it is *Peter* who makes an "unworthy" beggar and crippled man feel the wholeness and dignity of his life!

> 'Look at us!' Peter said to the man crippled from birth. The cripple gave him his whole attention, *hoping to get something*. Then Peter said: 'I have neither silver nor gold, *but what I have I give you!* In the name of Jesus Christ, the Nazorean, walk!' (Acts 3:4-6).

After this, Peter took the beggar by the hand and pulled him up, just he had been "pulled up" by Jesus. "Immediately, the beggar's feet and ankles became strong. He jumped up, stood for a moment, and then began to walk around" (vv. 7-8). Luke's portrait of Jesus, in both the gospel and in the Acts, inspires courage and confidence in his needy people today. He will always walk with those who call out to him. He will lift them up, free them from fear, and enable them to walk with him, on his way. His healing word to Peter was transforming. Peter learned from his journey with Jesus how to communicate that same healing transformation to others, like the crippled man. Luke's Jesus invites all his followers to move on with him, with heads held high, with dignity!

His Gentle Touch of Life

Only Luke preserves the gospel account of Jesus' meeting with the widow of Naim (7:11-17). This brief encounter is another part of Luke's gospel portrait which reveals the heart of his Jesus. Luke invites his readers to join Jesus' first disciples, a large crowd, and the widowed mother of an only son at Naim (vv. 11-12). There they witness the gentle touch of Jesus' power, which Luke knew so well. "Upon seeing her, the Lord was moved with pity and said to her, 'Do not cry' " (v.13). How human this Jesus is! Instead of waiting until someone expresses trust in him, he reaches into the depths of a grieving mother's sadness with the words: "Do not cry." He lets her know that "he knows." In the midst of hopeless situations, Christians can count on hearing the same gentle compassion from his lips. Moreover, his life-giving actions back up his words. Luke continues: "Jesus stepped forward, touched the litter, saying 'Young man, I bid you get up.' The dead man sat up and began to speak. Then Jesus gave him back to his mother " (vv. 14-15).

This is how "God visits his people" (v. 16), says the crowd *and* Luke: speaking words of comfort to those who need comfort; giving life to the lifeless; giving joy and hope back to the church, even when its life seems crushed out.

In the name of the risen Jesus, Paul would likewise give life to those with drooping spirits. In Acts 20:7-12, Paul gathered the Christian community of Troas together in prayer. He had been preaching for a very long time, when a young boy, Eutychus, fell from the upstairs window sill, where he had been drowsily listening to Paul. His friends knew the boy was dead. Still, they and the whole church hear:

> 'Do not be alarmed. There is life in him.' Afterwards, Paul went upstairs again, broke bread, and ate. He talked on for a long time — until dawn, when he departed. To the great comfort of the people, they were able to take the boy away alive.

Luke portrays Jesus not only as one who gives life and comfort, but also as one who enables others to do so. Peter and Paul were touched by Jesus. They, in turn, touched others. Jesus touches his church today. He enables his twentieth century disciples to be like him, and to say to a world full of fear: "Do not be afraid or alarmed. Get up. There is life here. God means to visit his people with new hope. He means to give back to you the life which you feared you had lost."

His Loving Embrace

The preceding and subsequent chapters of this guide to Luke-Acts deal in detail with the many sides of Jesus' special, "Lucan" personality, his vision, his attitudes, and his passionate love of the more needy among God's people. In his parable of tender mercy, often called "the prodigal son" (15:11-32), Luke not only reveals the kind of person Jesus is, but also the very heart of God, the Father. "God has indeed visited his people," in Jesus (7:16)!

In the familiar and much beloved story of the younger son, who had gone his sinful way (vv. 11-19), Jesus tells how "deeply moved" the father was upon seeing his son, "afar off." He rushed out to embrace him, even before the boy could finish his "prepared speech" of repentance (vv. 20f.). Christians often approach God with such an awareness of their sinfulness and shame that they forget who God really is. Luke reminds them. In Jesus, one can encounter "the Father," who is rich in compassion and eager to rejoice.

> Quick! Bring out the finest robe and put it on him. Put a ring on his finger and shoes on his feet. Take the fatted calf and kill it. Let us eat and celebrate, because this son of mine was dead and has come back to life. He was lost and is found! (vv. 22-24).

The father's loving embrace speaks louder than any words. This is the way Jesus shows God's true feelings toward his people! In their encounter with Luke's Jesus, Christians are welcomed, not punished. They meet Jesus as he is, the image of God, the Father, who embraces them with love.

Conclusion: A Final Loving Look

Luke's portrait of Jesus makes him a most desirable companion for the Christian journey. The meetings with Peter, with the widow of Naim, and with the forgiving father, reveal a Jesus who bestows dignity and life. One final "loving look," at the moment of Jesus' impending death, shows to what extremes Luke goes to invite confidence in his compassionate Lord.

Only Luke records the special moment when "Jesus turned around and looked at Peter" (22:61), after Peter had denied him. This glance first caused Peter to remember Jesus' prediction: "Before the cock crows today, you will deny me three times" (22:34, 61). Then it brought tears and sorrow: "He went out and wept bitterly" (v. 62). It is to this moment that Christians can attribute a repentant Peter's readiness to meet and rejoice in his *risen* Lord: "The Lord has been raised! It is true! He has appeared to Simon!" (24:34). Likewise, it was this look that would sustain Peter in his courageous efforts throughout the Acts of the Apostles!

When twentieth century Christians stand with Peter in his first and last encounters with the earthly Jesus (5:1-11 and 22:61-62), they allow the consoling word and forgiving look of Jesus to be the sustaining word and look of their whole lives. Such a Jesus as Luke presents is the most desirable companion one could hope for on the journey through life to the eternal embrace of the Father.

In the following chapters of this book, many of Luke's "themes for the journey" are considered for the sake of involving Christian pilgrims with Jesus' way more concretely. Since Luke's gospel has often been referred to as "the gospel of prayer," it is to this theme that we turn first.

Part II

The Lucan School of Discernment

1

ON PRAYER

> His reputation continued to grow, and large crowds would gather to hear him and to have their sickness cured. But he would always go off to some place *where he could be alone and pray*. (5:15f.).

While a quick paging through all four gospels makes it evident that Jesus was *the* model of "the prayerful person," a closer study of Luke's gospel makes it even clearer that Luke has Jesus pray the most. Not only does Luke's Jesus pray more, he is also more insistent that his disciples learn how to pray. Luke invites his readers to go off with Jesus, to become students in his "school of prayer."

The Discerning Prayer of Jesus

Of the four evangelists, only Luke has Jesus pray before every major event of his public life. In contemporary terms, Luke presents Jesus as a "person of discernment." After his baptism, Jesus is found at prayer, opening himself to the Holy Spirit and to the word of his Father in heaven: "You are my beloved son. On you my favor rests" (3:21f.). Before Jesus selects his twelve apostles, Luke alone has Jesus "go out to the mountain and pray, spending the night in communion with God" (6:12). Prior to the critical questioning of Peter and the disciples at Caesarea Philippi ("Who do you say that I am?"), it is only in Luke's gospel that we learn that Jesus had been "praying in seclusion" (9:18). And by the time Luke's readers arrive at the transfiguration event, they can almost expect that Luke's Jesus will "go up the mountain *in order to pray*" (9:28)!

One of the most revealing moments of Jesus' discerning prayer is his "time of agony" in the garden (22:39-46). Luke "frames" his agony scene with two similar warnings of Jesus for his disciples: "Pray that you may not be put to the test" (v. 40), and "Why are you sleeping? Wake up and pray that you may not be subjected to the trial" (v. 46). Between these two "teaching moments," Jesus practices what he preaches. He himself goes off, "about a stone's throw from them," in order to be tested. He is faced with "the cup" and he does not want to drink from it. His prayer response is: "Father, if it is your will, take this cup from me; yet, not my will, but yours be done" (v. 42). The immediate result of Jesus' prayer, found only in Luke's version of this scene, is the appearance of an angel to strengthen him (v. 43). But the agony is not over yet! "In his anguish, *he prayed with all the greater intensity*, and his sweat became like drops of blood falling to the ground" (v. 44). Although Jesus' intimate, intense communion with his Father leads him ahead with trust to the cup of his cross, the disciples do not yet understand the lesson in Jesus' example. For when Jesus arose from prayer, "he found them alseep, exhausted with grief" (v. 45). Luke's "framing" of the agony scene with calls to watchful prayer is, more than anything else, a sharp challenge to his readers of the early church and today. They are invited to watch how his lesson of discerning prayer will *gradually* be learned, as the light of the Holy Spirit guides the disciples after Jesus' resurrection. They will thereby come to know how to discern their Father's will in the critical moments of their lives, as Jesus and his disciples before them. However much the apostles failed him at first, and however much they would be disappointed by the crucifixion, they did learn enough to be open to their risen Lord, in prayer. Consequently, Luke's first volume ends, appropriately enough, with Jesus' disciples "in the temple constantly, speaking the praises of God" (24:53). Furthermore, the effects of Jesus' "school of prayer" will become evident in the prayer life of the church, as it unfolds throughout the pages of the Acts of the Apostles.

Jesus' "School of Prayer"

Luke's Jesus not only prays more than the Jesus of Mark, Matthew, or John, he also takes the time to train his disciples in the way to pray. In two concentrated sections of his gospel, at 10:38-11:13 and 18:1-14, Luke responds to the request made by Jesus' disciples: "Lord, teach us to pray, as John taught his disciples" (11:1).

The Our Father appears only in two of the four gospels, in Matthew 6:9-13 and in Luke 11:2-4. This is *the* way to pray. These are *the* words and sentiments to use when addressing God, the Father. It is the simple, direct, and personal prayer of Jesus himself, appropriated by the Christian community since the beginning. While Matthew "surrounds" his version of the Our Father by a caution against hypocrisy in prayer (Mt 6:5-8) and by an emphatic repetition of "forgive us as we forgive others" (Mt 6:14-15), Luke frames Jesus ' Our Father with 1) a lesson in how best to prepare to meet the Lord in prayer (10:38-42) and 2) a lesson in persistence (11:5-13).

The story of Jesus' encounter with Martha and Mary (10:38-42) begins with Martha's words of welcome. "She was busy with all the details of hospitality, when she said to Jesus: 'Lord, are you not concerned that my sister has left me to do the household tasks all alone?' " (v. 40). Now, Martha was as good a person as here sister Mary was. However, she, like so many good Christians, had "not seen the forest for the trees." In her anxiety to make the Lord welcome, she had become lost in the work and details. "Martha, Martha," Jesus replied, "you are anxious and upset about many things; one thing only is required. Mary has chosen the better portion, and she shall not be deprived of it" (v. 41f.). And what was the "one thing required," the "better portion," the best way to welcome the Lord? Luke tells us that Mary "seated herself at the Lord's feet and listened to his words" (v. 39). In this way, Luke teaches all his "students of prayer and discipleship" that "the best way to pray" is to be well disposed, that is, to choose to be present with the Lord and open to him, as he speaks. This receptive attitude in prayer might be expressed in this way: "What is the

Lord's agenda for me, right now?" Consequently, instead of "running ahead of the Lord," Christians do the "best thing" in prayer when they pray as Mary did. In a very real sense, Luke's Jesus is a teacher like Eli, the priest and teacher of old (see 1 Sam 3:1-18). That holy man, having learned from a long life of service to the Lord, would sum up for his "student," Samuel, the heart of what prayer union with God is: "Samuel, go to sleep, and if you are called, reply 'Speak, Lord, your servant is listening' " (1 Sam 3:9). Samuel did as his teacher said. He became a renowned prophet of the Lord, one who came to know the mind of the Lord for himself and for his people. By presenting the Martha and Mary account as he does, Luke gives his readers the basic lesson in prayer: "When you pray, say 'Speak Lord, your servant is listening'. Let *his* word reverberate deep within. *Then respond* 'Father, hallowed be your name, your kingdom come. Give us each day our daily bread. Forgive us our sins for we too forgive all who do us wrong; and subject us not to the trial' " (11:2-4, Luke's version of the *Our Father*).

Immediately after Jesus teaches his disciples the Father prayer, he presents a cluster of stories and sayings that underline the need for *persistence in prayer*. The first is like a photo that speaks louder than many words.

> If one of you knows someone who comes to him in the middle of the night and says to him, 'Friend, lend me three loaves, for a friend of mine has come in from a journey and I have nothing to offer him'; and he from inside should reply, 'Leave me alone. The door is shut now and my children and I are in bed. I cannot get up to look after your needs'— I tell you, even though he does not get up and take care of the man because of friendship, *he will do so because of his persistence, and give him as much as he needs.* (11:5-8).

"So," says Luke's Jesus, even though you sometimes wonder if the Lord is hearing your prayer, "ask and you shall receive; seek and you shall find; knock and it shall be opened to you. For whoever asks, receives; whoever seeks, finds; whoever knocks, is admitted" (11:9f.). The God of Luke's Jesus is more than a friend. He is truly a father. In fact, he is a father who gives much more than any earthly father can give! Luke ends this "mini-section" on *how to pray* with these striking question-statements:

> What father among you will give his child a snake if he asks for a fish, or hand her a scorpion if she asks for an egg? If you, with all your sins, know how to give your children good things, *how much more will the heavenly Father give the Holy Spirit to those who ask him*? (11:11-13).

Persistence in prayer pays off for the students in Jesus' school of prayer, because their God is their generous father!

Luke's Jesus reemphasizes the "pay off" of persistent prayer with two parable stories in chapter 18. At the end of the account of the widow woman, who insists on her rights from the unjust judge (vv. 1-8), Jesus says: "To those who call out to him, day and night, God will give swift justice" (vv. 7-8). Luke's readers can conclude, once more, that God is indeed a faithful God! It is truly worth the effort to "pray always without losing heart" (v. 1)!

A final vivid "lesson in prayer," following immediately upon this story, sums up all the previous lessons Luke has laid out for his Christian faith community.

> Jesus then spoke this parable addressed to those who believed in their own self-righteousness while holding everyone else in contempt: 'Two men went up to the temple to pray; one was a

> Pharisee, the other a tax collector. The Pharisee with head unbowed prayed in this fashion: 'I give you thanks, O God, that I am not like the rest of men — grasping, crooked, adulterous — or even like this tax collector. . . . The other man kept his distance, not even daring to raise his eyes to heaven. All he did was beat his breast and say, 'O God, be merciful to me, a sinner." (18:9-13).

As the parable concludes, Jesus says that the tax collector's prayer was heard: "He went home justified, while the other man did not. For everyone who exalts himself shall be humbled, while those who humble themselves shall be exalted" (18:14).

The key to the tax collector's prayer is *humility*. He knows who he is, a sinner. He knows who God is, mercy personified. He *is himself* in his prayer. He lets God be himself. And he leaves it at that, trusting that God will be merciful toward him. Indeed, as Luke reports, he *exalted* him! And the same merciful God will exalt all of his children, says Luke, who pray with openness, with persistence, and with humility. "Speak, Father, for your children are listening. We are knocking at the door, and we know we will be admitted. We give you thanks, O God, that we are 'like the rest' of your needy children. Into your hands we commend our spirits."

Prayer Among God's Faithful: In the Infancy Story, the Acts, Today

Along with Jesus' promise of his Father's faithfulness to his people. Luke also adds a challenge of Jesus for all his people to be faithful: "When the Son of Man comes, will he find any faith on the earth?" (18:8). This final verse of the "persistent widow story" leads Luke's readers into the worlds of his infancy narrative, his Acts, and his hearers across the centuries.

When the Son of Man came for the first time, according to the birth story of Luke, he *did* find faith on the earth. It was a lived faith, embodied in persons of prayer (in Luke's Journey A, Faithful Israel). When he came again in the person of the Holy Spirit (in Luke's Journey C, the Apostolic Church), he found more faith, a faith manifested in those disciples who light up the pages of the Acts of the Apostles. After travelling with the people to whom Jesus came as a child and in the Spirit, it will be even easier for those who travel on Journey D (the Church-in-time until the end) to let Luke's inspired message color their prayer lives today.

Luke presents the story of Jesus' incarnation in such a way that no reader can miss the prayerful atmosphere into which he was born. Five "faithful children of Israel" are there to receive him, prayerfully. Zechariah hears from the angel, Gabriel, that "Your prayer has been heard, and your wife Elizabeth will bear a son, whom you will call John" (1:13). Although Zechariah was struck dumb because of his initial lack of trust ("How am I to know this? I am an old man; my wife too is advanced in age," 1:18), he soon uttered a prayer, full of trust and praise, known to the church as "Zechariah's Canticle" (1:67-79). His wife, Elizabeth, is another person of prayer, who welcomes Jesus in prayer: "Blest are you among women and blest is the fruit of your womb" (1:42). Truly blest, most of all, is she "who trusted that the Lord's words to her would be fulfilled" (1:45), namely, Mary. For she would be the most prayerful person of all, "treasuring all these things and reflecting on them in her heart" (2:19 & 51)! Two final "infancy characters," Simeon and Anna (2:25-40), enfold the child and the holy family in an embrace of prayerful peace and thanksgiving.

Turning to the journey of the church in Acts, Luke's readers find almost a mirror reflection back on Jesus and the prayerful ambience of the infancy narrative. In the very first chapter of the Acts they learn that the first post-resurrection apostle was chosen after prayerful discernment. "Together they devoted themselves to constant prayer" (Acts 1:12f.), and their prayer was:

> O Lord, you read the hearts of all. Make known to us which of these two (Joseph or Matthias) you choose for this apostolic ministry (replacing Judas). (Acts 1:24).

Later, in Acts 6, the choice of the first seven deacons was done in order that the ministry of the word *and prayer* might be carried on more faithfully (Acts 6:4).

According to St. Augustine, "If Stephen had not prayed, the church would not have had Paul." Luke, of course, makes it clear that Paul's conversion was the work of Jesus himself, on the road to Damascus (Acts 9). Still, what began at Stephen's martyrdom would flower in the prayer life of the apostle to the Gentiles! Moreover, Stephen's word-for-word imitation of Jesus' own prayer at his death shows Paul and the church-in-time *the* way to face death, prayerfully:

> As Stephen was being stoned, he could be heard praying, 'Lord Jesus, receive my spirit.' He fell to his knees and cried out in a loud voice, 'Lord, do not hold this sin against them.' And with that he died. (Acts 7:59f.).

Stephen's echo of Jesus' prayer of trust in death is Luke's way of inviting his readers to the same radical trust in God. (See Lk 23:32-46 for parallels.)

Christians in the twentieth century might respond that Stephen and the apostles were so close to Jesus that their imitation of his life and prayer was expected of them. However, Luke makes it obvious that such a spirit of prayerful discernment is for *all*, especially as he presents the example of two prayerful "outsiders," Cornelius and Lydia.

In Acts 10, Luke's readers encounter Cornelius, a centurion of the Roman cohort at Caesarea. He was not an apostle or a deacon. In fact, he was not even a Jew or Christian. Nonetheless, because of his "generosity and constant prayer to God" and because he was "a religious, God-fearing man" (10:1f), his prayer was heard and his generosity was remembered by God (10:31). And upon Cornelius and his whole household descended the Holy Spirit (10:44). Later, in Acts 16, Lydia arrives on the scene. She was not among the first women to follow Jesus (see Lk 8:1-3). She was merely "a dealer in purple goods from the town of Thyatira," who opened her home to Paul on his way. But she did so because she had first opened herself up to God, joining the women who were gathered "by the bank of the river, which Paul thought would be a good place of prayer" (16:13). Luke indicates that Lydia "already reverenced God, and that the Lord opened her heart to accept what Paul was saying" (v. 14).

The way Luke "dots the pages" of Journeys A and C (Faithful Israel and the Apostolic Church) with all kinds of people of prayer can be a source of inspiration for twentieth century Christians of all states of life. *Anyone* can "put on Christ!" *Everyone* is called to be a person of prayer, according to the mind and heart of Luke's Jesus!

Two More Lucan Ways to Pray, Today

Christians who want to pray better today can pause after their journey through Luke-Acts to : 1) choose one or two characters from Luke's writings with whom they identify the most; and 2) pray the "Prayer of the Church," the Liturgy of the Hours, which includes not only the psalms, but also all of Luke's canticles (Mary's Magnificat, Zechariah's Canticle, Simeon's "Now, Lord, you can dismiss your servant"). By so doing, they join the praying faithful of the past and present in making holy each day of their lives.

For example, one might chose Mary and/or Zechariah as "prayer partners" and ask: In the light of how they responded to the unbelievable news of the births of John and Jesus, how do I respond in times of surprise, crisis, or confusion? Is it with fear and awe? Then I am like the both of them. Do I let God tell me "not to fear?" And where does that gentle whisper lead me? To immediate trust and joyful sharing of God's good news? Then I am like Mary: "Let it be done to me according to your word" (1:38); "My spirit finds joy in God my Savior" (1:47). Or is my response more hesitant, more gradual? Then I feel more like Zechariah, who could not believe at first. He could not speak at all, in fact, until he had seen some of God's promises fulfilled. Then he burst forth with "Blessed be the Lord, the God of Israel, because he has visited and ransomed his people" (1:68). Both modes of responding are human and real, suggests Luke. It is up to his readers to accept who they are in relationship with God and how they find themselves in prayer, now. Then it is up to them to choose "their best way to pray," just as Mary did, "treasuring all these things and reflecting on them in her heart" (2:19).

Today's readers of the Acts also profit from reflecting: Which of the "star characters" in Acts am I like, in regard to prayer? Am I *generous and open to the word of God,* like Lydia and Cornelius? Do I have any of the courage that Paul manifested in the midst of the horrible storm at sea (in Acts 27:21-26): "Last night a messenger of the God whose man I am, and whom I serve, stood by me and said 'Don't be afraid, Paul.' So, keep up your courage, men. I trust in God that it will all work out just as I have been told" (v. 24f.)? By whatever Lucan character one plans to measure his or her prayer, it is certainly Luke's intention that the *primary focus* of attention be put on Jesus, *the* person of prayer. And so contemporary prayer people do best to identify with him and hear this final teaching of his:

> Consider the ravens: they do not sow or reap, they have neither cellar nor barn, yet God feeds them. How much more important you are than the birds! Which of you, by worrying, can add a moment to your life span? Stop worrying!! The unbelievers of this world are always running after what they are to eat and to drink. Your Father knows you need such things. Seek out his kingship over you and the rest will follow in turn. (12:24-31).

One last practical means of putting on the Lucan spirit of prayer is to pray the "prayer of the church," that is, to join with other Christian men and women, who pray the church's Liturgy of the Hours, daily. The experience of this part of the Catholic Church's liturgy, which used to be seen as an obligation of the ordained priest alone, is now happily being celebrated by many baptized faithful. With the help of this structured arrangement of psalms, scripture readings and canticles, they make holy the various hours of the day. For example, the church's "morning prayer" consists of an opening hymn, several psalms, a brief scripture passage, and Zechariah's Canticle "Blessed be the Lord, the God of Israel" (Lk 1:67-79). At midday, there are usually two psalms and a verse of scripture to nourish the praying Christian "half way through" his or her work day. At "evening prayer" Mary's Canticle, her Magnificat (Lk 1:46-55), follows the psalms and scripture reading. And finally, before bed, the official "night prayer" of the church features Simeon's Canticle, "Now, Lord, you can dismiss your servant in peace" (Lk 2:29). Simeon's prayer, along with one psalm, serves as *the* trusting way for the church to end its day and prepare for sleep.

Anyone who is interested in praying the church's Liturgy of the Hours alone (in spiritual union with people throughout the world), or with others (e.g., with a spouse, with family or friends), can easily acquire volume and learn how to pray "with the church." Praying with God's church and his word in this way can be a challenging and rewarding means for the twentieth century Christian community to become more "of one mind and of one heart" (Acts 4:32).

Such a daily practice of praying with the psalms and the church might even lead Christians to an experience of God and Jesus similar to that of Augustine, who expresses it this way:

> God praised himself (in the psalms) so that we might give him fitting praise; because God chose to praise himself, we found the way in which to bless God . . . . How I wept when I heard your hymns and canticles, being deeply moved by the sweet singing of your church. Those voices flowed into my ears, truth filtered into my heart, and from my heart surged waves of devotion. Tears ran down, and I was happy in my tears . . . . It is your voice I hear in every psalm, the voice of praise, of suffering, of joyful expectation, of present distress.

2

ONE IN THE SPIRIT

Some forty years before Luke described the Christian community as "one in mind and heart" through prayer (Acts 4:32), St. Paul had already expressed the source of that unity in vivid terms: it was *through the Holy Spirit* that Christians were strengthened inwardly and united with Christ and with each other.

> May he (the Father) strengthen you inwardly *through the working of his Spirit.* May Christ dwell in your hearts through faith, and may charity be the root and foundation of your life. Thus you will be able to grasp fully the breadth and length and height and depth of Christ's love, and experience this love which surpasses all knowledge, so that you may attain to the fullness of God himself. (Eph 3:17-19).

Paul called upon his Ephesian brothers and sisters to act in accord with the Spirit-gift that was theirs.

> I plead with you to live a life worthy of the calling you have received, with perfect humility, meekness, and patience, bearing with one another lovingly. Make every effort to preserve *the unity which has the Spirit as its binding force.* (Eph 4:1-3).

Paul had thus articulated much of the theology of the Holy Spirit that guides the church today. Christians are God's children because the Spirit of God dwells in them (Romans 8:14-16). It is the Spirit who teaches them how to pray (Romans 8:26-27) and it is "in the Spirit" that they have a sure hope of eternal life (Romans 8:17-25 and 5:1-11). However clearly Paul had described the power and importance of the Spirit in the Christian life, it was left to the evangelist Luke to express in his gospel and Acts narrative the "how it all came to be 'in the Spirit.' " Mark and Matthew, writing about the same time as Luke, hardly mention the Spirit. John, who wrote after Luke, continues to develop the first century understanding of the Spirit at work among Christians. But it is Luke who first traces the way that the Spirit of God guided the Christian community from the beginning. This chapter is meant to bring out several key elements in the dominant role which the Spirit played in the formation of the Christian community. Such "facts" will hopefully enable Luke's readers of the twentieth century to let the Spirit guide them ever more authentically in their desire to be one in mind and heart.

The "Facts" Concerning the Spirit in Luke-Acts

"The Spirit of the Lord is upon me," says Jesus in his inaugural mission statement (4:18). "The Holy Spirit will teach you all that should be said" is Jesus' message to his disciples, mid-way through his earthly ministry (12:12). His final words to his followers, at the time of his ascension are: "See, I send down upon you the promise of my Father. Remain here in the city until you are clothed with power from on high" (24:49). From the beginning until the end of his journey on earth, Jesus was guided by the Spirit. That Spirit, which had descended upon him "in visible form like a dove" (3:22), led him into the desert for forty days (4:1) and would lead him to his life-giving death. It is most important that Luke's readers become aware that *only Jesus* was blessed by this Spirit during his earthly ministry. The importance of this "Lucan twist" will become evident when the work of the Spirit is unveiled in the infancy narrative and in the life of the early church.

Even in the opening chapters of his gospel, before Jesus begins his active ministry, the Spirit has the spotlight. "John will be filled by the Holy Spirit" (1:15). The Spirit overshadows Mary (1:34). Elizabeth was filled with the Spirit (1:42), as was Zechariah (1:67). Simeon, too, was blessed with the Spirit, who "revealed to him that he would not experience death until he had seen the Anointed of the Lord" (2:26f.). Luke thus makes it very clear that the Spirit had prepared the way for Jesus, by conditioning those who would first receive him. Moreover, by the way the Spirit worked in them, Luke gives his readers obvious hints as to how the Spirit continues to work in them. For example, those who are blessed with the Spirit in Luke's infancy narrative share that Spirit with others. Mary, Zechariah, and Simeon all proclaim the goodness of God, for the sake of those who are around them. Elizabeth hears from Mary that God will reveal himself in mercy, "to confuse the proud and to raise the lowly to high places"

(1:46-55). Zechariah would dispel the fear of those around him by proclaiming that Jesus was coming to give his people a knowledge of salvation, in freedom from their sins, to show them the kindness of God, to shine on those who sit in darkness, and to guide their feet in the way of peace (1:76-79). By way of anticipation, Simeon would proclaim "good news" to all peoples, for Jesus was to be "a revealing light to the Gentiles" as well as "the glory of his people Israel" (2:30-32). In the infancy narrative of Luke, the Spirit of God is a gift to be shared, a proclamation of God's mercy and peace to all peoples!

In the life of the early church, according to the Acts of the Apostles, Luke further explains the function of the Spirit in the Christian community. Once the community is baptized with the Holy Spirit (Acts 1:5 and 2:1-4), it will be able to act and to teach as Jesus did. "Clothed with the power from on high," the Christian family will *be Jesus* in the world. For now, the Spirit that had been only his, was upon them! As Luke describes it, from the time of Pentecost (Acts 2), all the major characters of the Acts are driven by the Spirit to act and to preach boldly. Peter, who had wept after denying Jesus three times in the courtyard (Luke 22:54-62), suddenly proclaims God's message with utter courage before his Jewish brothers and sisters:

> You made use of pagans to crucify and kill him. God, however, raised and freed him from death's bitter pains and raised him up again. . . . Once exalted at God's right hand, Jesus first received the promised Holy Spirit from the Father and then poured out this Spirit upon us. (Acts 2:23f. & 33).

Peter and John were imprisoned for their courageous sermons, which featured "the new way of reform" and baptism for the forgiveness of sins (Acts 2:38). Yet, they stood fast, "filled with the Holy Spirit" (Acts 4:8). Upon their release from prison, the entire Christian community "was filled with the Holy Spirit and continued to speak God's word with confidence" (Acts 4:31). Therefore, in the mind of Luke, the boldness of the Spirit was contagious. Stephen also had "caught the Spirit." His eloquent "story of salvation" sermon (in Acts 7) angered its Jewish hearers unto murder. However, Stephen was so filled with the Holy Spirit that he forgave his murderers, as he handed over his own spirit to his Lord (Acts 7:59-60). Courage and mercy marked the life of the early church, driven by the Spirit! The Spirit of the Lord also "snatched Philip away" from Samaria and brought him to Azotus. There he went about *boldly* "announcing the good news in all the towns until he had reached Caesarea" (Acts 8:39-40). The same Spirit of courage compelled Paul to go to Jerusalem, not knowing what would happen there, except that "the Holy Spirit has been warning me from city to city that chains and hardships await me" (Acts 20:22-23).

The Holy Spirit was not only poured out on the first *Jewish* disciples. In Luke's "second Pentecost" (in Acts 10), the circumcised Jews were surprised that the gift of the Spirit had also been bestowed upon *Gentiles*, namely, upon Cornelius and his entire household (Acts 10:45-46)! The marvelous good news for all Luke's faithful readers is that the Holy Spirit *is meant for all people*, for anyone who obeys God with an open heart (see also Acts 5:32). In fact Paul's final words say it best.

> The Holy Spirit has stated it well when he said to your fathers through the prophet Isaiah: 'Go to this people and say, 'You may listen intensely yet you will never understand; you

> may look intently, yet you will never see . . . . Now you must realize that this salvation of God has been transmitted to the Gentiles — who will heed it! (Acts 28:25f., & 28).

This "final word" of Paul brings to completion Luke's account of the Acts of the Apostles. In its harsh tone toward "this people" (i.e., Israel, the first loved by God, who had grown sluggish, Acts 28:27), Luke gives his explanation for the church's early mission to the non-Jew. However, his final word must be heard in its context, for in the overall setting of Luke's final chapter 28, it becomes clear that Paul's harsh sounding words are not aimed at *all* the Jewish people. Indeed, Paul is preaching this very sermon to "prominent members of the Jewish community" at Rome, whom he addresses as "my brothers" (Acts 28:17). He says that he wears his chains "solely because he shares the hope of Israel" (28:20). These Jewish leaders are "anxious to hear him present his views" (28:23) and although some would not believe, others were "even convinced by what he said" (Acts 28:24). Paul's good news about Jesus is for everyone, says Luke, for everyone who is open to the power of God's word and Spirit, no matter whether they are Gentile or Jew.

These "Spirit facts" bring the reader of Luke-Acts to several obvious conclusions about the role of the Spirit in their lives as Christians. First, it is the Spirit of the Lord that enlightens their hearts, making them receptive to God's mercy and conversion. Secondly, with the Spirit of the Lord upon them through baptism, all Christians are blessed with boldness and courage to share that gift with others, by loving word and action. Finally, the gifts of the Spirit are meant for all peoples, thereby driving baptized Christians out of any small circles of faith which they might find themselves in. In point of fact, the

Pentecost promise is meant for them: "You have received great power when the Holy Spirit came down upon you; consequently, you are to be my witnesses in Jerusalem, throughout Judea and Samaria, yes, even to the ends of the earth" (Acts 1:7f.).

Putting "The Facts" into Act: Today

In the previous chapter of this book, St. Augustine was quoted as saying "without Stephen's prayer, the church would not have had Paul." In this application of Luke's message concerning the role of the Spirit in the church's life today, one might paraphrase Augustine in this way: "without Luke's gospel and Acts, the church would not have had such a vivid understanding of the Spirit at work in its midst." Twentieth century Christians thank Luke for his gift to them best when they actualize his inspired message in their lives today. The way for contemporary followers of Jesus to do this is to accept the Spirit of God in their own lives, in prayerful discernment of God's will for them.

One helpful means to assist Christians in the discernment process is that offered by St. Ignatius of Loyola and those who continue his way of "discerning the spirits." When Christians find themselves in confusion or at a moment of critical decision making, they can cooperate with the Spirit of God within them by prayerfully pausing to line up, in writing, the many thoughts and feelings they are experiencing in their present situation. They are then wise to list all the possible options for action that seem open to them. Thus, instead of waiting passively for some lightning flash of inspiration from

God, they can ask themselves and God: "Which of these various 'ways to go' is it that God might want? Where is it that the Spirit is leading me? As I meditate seriously upon each option for action, what do I feel? Is it a sense of peace or an aura of darkness that covers my heart? Do I experience God's mercy or some bitter revulsion?" When Christians dialogue with God about their minds' honest thoughts and their hearts' deepest feelings, they allow the Spirit of God to lead them as they are, *as whole Christian persons*. In this way, they will sense the presence of Jesus at their sides, lovingly assisting them in their desire to do his Father's will. They will begin to value their lives in the world as if through the very eyes of Jesus himself!

It is by such an attempt at prayerful discernment, along with further means offered by Ignatius and other spiritual guides, that Christians today can come closer to perceiving God's way for them. So enlightened by the Spirit, they will move on with ever more confidence to the next stages of the journey that lie before them. Ignatius' way is one way that can help Luke's readers to discern God's will. It is to the theme of "doing God's will" that the readers of this book now turn, always under the guidance of the Holy Spirit.

3

ON "DOING GOD'S WILL"

In regard to "doing God's will," more Christians than are ready to admit it are very much like St. Paul. They want to do what God wills. They say "Thy will be done." But it often takes a crisis before they realize that they, at least unconsciously, have long been in pursuit of having their own wills accomplished. This seems to have been the case with St. Paul. When he reviews his conversion experience before his own people in Jerusalem, he says: "I was a staunch defender of God, just as all of you are today. Furthermore, I persecuted this new way to the point of death. I arrested and imprisoned both men and women" (Acts 22:3f.). Then Paul met Jesus: "Saul, Saul, why do you persecute me?" (v. 7). He came to realize that God's will was different than he had thought. And he concludes:

> A certain Ananias, a devout observer of the law and well spoken of by all the Jews who lived in Damascus, came and stood by me and said, 'Saul, recover your sight.' In that instant I regained my sight and looked at him. The next thing he said was, 'The God of our fathers long ago designated you to know his will, to look upon the Just One, and to hear the sound of his voice: before all you are to be his witness to what you have seen and heard. (Acts 22:12-15).

In the pages that follow, Luke's readers will be challenged to examine their real experience and understanding of "doing God's will."

Your Will Be Done

Surprisingly, Luke's version of the Lord's Prayer (11:2-4) does *not* include the petition "Your will be done" (see Mt 6:10). One might well wonder why this central theme in Judeo-Christian spirituality is missing here. Perhaps it is because Luke wants his "co-travellers" not only to *say* "your will be done" but also to *do* it. Perhaps Luke has chosen to incorporate the prfound meaning of these words into the lives of his characters in the gospel and Acts. (In fact, more than any other gospel writer, Luke is explicitly concerned that his community of faith do God's will, according to the heart and mind of Jesus. There are some 9 references to God's "will," "purpose," "intention" in Luke-Acts, at 1:38, 7:30, 22:42, Acts 2:23, 13:22, 26, 18:21, 20:27, 21:14, and 22:14. This is not to mention the many closely related urgings of Luke to "listen to God's word and act upon it," e.g., in 8:21.) By examining three passages carefully, Luke's readers today can be assisted in their desire to be dedicated to God's will, as Mary, Jesus, and Paul were.

The first time Luke refers to God's will in his gospel comes from the heart and lips of Mary: "I am the servant of the Lord. Let it be done to me as you say" (1:38). Mary's response to the angel, upon receiving the awesome message about Jesus' birth, is so familiar and significant to all believers that it hardly needs more than a mention here. Yet, in Luke's overall scheme of his gospel and Acts, her dedication to what God says stands as a "signpost," not only in her life, but in the life of her son. It also proves to be an indication of things to come in the life of the church, which Mary comes to symbolize.

Luke's Jesus shows the truth of the phrase "like mother, like son," when, at the end of his ministry on earth, he proclaims in the garden of Gethsemane: "Father, if it is *your will*, take this cup from me; yet *not my will* but *yours* be done" (22:42). It is important to notice more than the similarity of the words that Mary and Jesus use. Luke also has both mother and son make their statements of trust in similar circumstances and with similar depths of emotion. For example, Mary is "deeply troubled" and confused by the angel's greeting and is told: "Do not fear, Mary, you have found favor with God" (1:29-30). Jesus is also in anguish over the cup he is about to drink, his death. Yet after he says "your will be done," "an angel appeared to him from heaven to strengthen him" (22:43). The suffering servant, Jesus, born of God and of Mary, learned well from the life-long union with his Father in heaven and with his mother on earth. His response in his moment of ultimate crisis is virtually the same as his mother's: "I am the servant of the Lord. Let it be done!"

Luke does not stop here in his conscious development of

this theme. Not only is "the son like the mother." In the Acts, "other sons and daughters become like their brother." This becomes vividly clear in the life and mission of Paul. When Paul has arrived near the end of his journey in Acts, he is confronted by a certain Agabus. This man had come from Judea to warn Paul of dangers ahead. He first took Paul's belt off, tied his own hands and feet with it, and said: "Thus says the Holy Spirit. This is how the Jews in Jerusalem will bind the owner of this belt and hand him over to the Gentiles" (Acts 21:11). Upon hearing this ominous warning of the Spirit, those who were with Paul urged him not to go to Jerusalem. How much like Jesus' disciples in the garden crisis are Paul's companions! They do not seem to have grasped the meaning of his life. Yet, when Paul questions them tenderly ("Why are you crying and breaking my heart this way? In the name of the Lord Jesus, I am prepared, not only for imprisonment, but for death!"), "they said nothing further except '*the Lord's will be done*' " (Acts 21:14). Like mother, like son! Like the son, his faithful followers!

Luke's writings are thus tied together by the strong cords of dedication to the will of God, even in the face of confusion, fear, and death itself. Mary is *the* model of Christian love and commitment, according to Luke, for she not only said "Let it be done as you say" (1:38), she also "heard the word of God and acted on it" (8:21). And like Mary, Jesus and his followers also discover life and freedom from fear, when they say *and do* God's will as it is manifested to them. Perhaps the readers of Luke can now respond to the question raised earlier ("Why does Luke *not* include the petition 'Your will be done' in his version of the Lord's Prayer?"). Is it not because he wants them to realize it is now "up to them," the living members of the Christian community, to be like the mother, like the son, and like all the faithful ones who have gone before them?

God's Will: A Crutch?

Several times in the history of the church-in-time (Journey D), the "will of God" has been used as an excuse to accomplish the distorted "will of man." The tragedy of Hitler's Germany is one vivid example of this. More often, without such obvious malice, uninformed Christians can also distort "the will of God." For example, in the face of great injustice or oppressive discrimination, good Christian people have thrown their hands up in the air, saying "this must be God's will!" They might have thought they were doing what Jesus did. But they might also have been using "God's will" as an escape from putting their hands to the plow and from involving themselves in the very relief of such situations. Luke's two-volume work does not allow for such misinterpretations or escapes. In fact, according to Luke, rank discrimination and injustice *does* call for God's will to be done. However, it is the dedication to doing something about such situations, however insignificant one's efforts might appear, that a Christian is "in tune" with God's will and desire to be active in the world.

Perhaps the Christian community's dependence on God's will is most often experienced in times of incurable sickness, untimely deaths, or serious harm done to people through senseless violence or freak accidents. When one is standing near the hospital or sick bed, there seems to be no way to help. There is nothing to say. A beloved person is dying or has died, or one's child has already been severly abused or injured by an accident. At these critical moments, Christians *do* God's will when they reach out to comfort the sick and the sad people around them. They say "the Lord's will be done" as Mary, Jesus, and Paul did, not so much in words as in recognizing God's healing presence in the present moment. For it is *now* that God wants to heal the wounds of hopelessness, anger, or sadness. "The living" do God's will by giving the life of comfort to the dying, by giving the embrace of assuring love to the broken. Such love-in-action speaks louder than a thousand words. It assures the needy that God is here now, in the embrace and presence of friends. To say "it must have been God's will" does not really help lift the spirits of those who are crushed. To take the initiative *to manifest* God's will and love for the bereaved: this is "doing God's will" in a most convincing way! Allowing the sick and suffering to express their feelings of grief, of anger with God or others, is much more of a healing gift than stifling their feelings with some words that might only add to the confusion and pain. God's will is not, and never was, "a crutch" for those "in tune" with God's real intentions for his people. It is "the heartbeat" of the Christian life. It is "the crux" of a Christian's experience with God on the journey.

"Let It Be Done": The Crux

Crux is the Latin word for cross. In the life of Jesus, the cross was the ultimate expression of God's will for him. He chose it, out of love for his people and his Father. God's will is also, to use the familiar expression in the English language, "the *crux* of the matter." What God wants for his people is the *crux* of the Christian life-project. The agenda for this project is not, however, some vague guesswork about what God might want. Luke, like the other three evangelists, was inspired by the Spirit of God to present to his people concrete modes of living out God's intention for them. Luke was thus inspired by the same Spirit of God, on *Journey D* (the church-in-time), as were the other characters of his two-volume work before him. The fruit of this inspiration follows in the other chapters of this book, which take up the specific concerns that Luke knew were at the heart of God's desire for his community. It is to four of the most urgent of those concerns that Luke's readers are now invited to turn their attention. What is God's will for his people? What is the *crux* of the Christian life, according to Luke? It lies in how Christians attend to the issues of: 1) the poor and the rich; 2) justice and peace; 3) women and men; and 4) God's mercy for the sinner.

Part III

Lucan Themes for the Journey

1

THE POOR AND THE RICH

In his gospel and Acts, Luke presents Jesus and his model disciples as persons filled with a special love for the poor. The very first sermon Luke's Jesus delivers begins with the passage of Isaiah:

> The Spirit of the Lord is upon me; therefore he has anointed me. He has sent me to bring glad tidings to the poor, to proclaim liberty to captives, recovery of sight to the blind, and release to prisoners. (4:18ff.).

Likewise, Jesus' famous "sermon on the level stretch" (6:17-49) makes obvious his predilection for the materially poor, especially when it is contrasted with Matthew's "sermon on the mount" (Mt 5:1-11). Where Matthew begins with the beatitude "How blest are *the poor in spirit;* the reign of God is theirs" (Mt 5:3), Luke's Jesus says "Blest are *you poor;* the reign of God is yours" (6:20). Then, when Luke adds a matching "Woe to *you rich,* for your consolation is now" (6:24), it becomes clearer to see with whom Luke's Jesus stands. He stands with and for the poorest among God's people! (None of Matthew's beatitudes are accompanied by woes. Likewise, his "first beatitude" concerning "the poor in spirit" can be understood to take in anyone who is needy and recognizes that their need, whatever it is, can be satisfied only by God.) Luke's adaptation of Jesus' earliest sermon lets his readers know that Jesus was addressing both the materially poor *and* the well-to-do of his time.

Later in his gospel, Luke shows that Jesus practiced what he preached. He would spend his time among the poor and with the outsider. He would "cut against the grain," not only in his time, but also in the lives of anyone who would hear him:

> Whenever you give a lunch or dinner, do not invite your friends or relatives or wealthy neighbors. They might invite you in return and thus repay you. No, when you have a reception, invite beggars and the cripples, the lame and the blind. You should be pleased that they cannot repay you, for you will be repaid in the resurrection of the just. (14:12-14).

Jesus addressed these words to a leading Pharisee who had invited him to dinner. Shortly thereafter, in "the parable of the large dinner" (14:16-23), Luke once again adds something to a story he shares with Matthew. (See Mt 22:9 in contrast with Lk 14:21, which brings out the Lucan emphasis, italicized here): "Go out quickly into the streets and alleys of the town and bring in *the poor and the crippled, the blind and the lame* . . . I want my house to be full." According to Luke, Jesus' first disciples would follow his example and preference for the poor by their sharing in a communal lifestyle and by "selling their property and goods, dividing everything on the basis of each one's need" (Acts 2:45). As a consequence, "there would be no one needy among them" (Acts 4:32ff.).

Luke's Message Is for Rich and Poor Alike

The emphasis in Luke's writings concerning the poor is truly "good news" for the poor. He assures them that their condition, like that of the beggar Lazarus (in the parable of "rich man, poor man," 16:19-31), will be dramatically changed. The poor will be the recipients of God's special blessings, because they are poor and needy. Their place "in the bosom of Abraham" (16:22) awaits them on that basis. At the same time, Luke did not write his two-volume work only for the poor to hear and react to. The same parable also features the selfish rich man, who "dressed in purple and linen, and feasted splendidly every day" (16:19). He stands for all people of means who fail to be generous. They will gain their appropriate negative inheritance: in "the abode of the dead, in torment, tortured by the flames" (16:23f.).

The surprisingly large number of Lucan examples and parables that concern money, greed, dependence on possessions, etc., makes it very likely that Luke had many well-to-do people among his hearers. There are at least twenty-five to thirty passages in his writings that are not found in the other gospels concerning these themes. Perhaps the Lucan church community could be fairly compared to the church of the United States today, which is made up of the very poor, the very rich, and many in between. Whatever the precise composition of his community was, Luke's purpose in reinforcing the traditional biblical obligation to be detached from earthly possessions and to share them with the poor is as relevant for today's believer as it was in the first Christian century. No doubt it was in the spirit of this concern of God for the poor of all times that such people as Francis of Assisi, Vincent de Paul, and many others in the history of Christianity, gave up what they had in order to share their lives with the poor. In today's world and church, Luke calls people of all economic levels to hear God's challenging message and to respond like those "holy ones" who have preceded them on the journey with Jesus.

The Message for "Those-Who-Have"

From the beginning of his gospel, Luke's Jesus prods "those who have more than others" to be generous. Even before Jesus begins his public ministry, one hears John the Baptizer giving the following concrete means of reform to his newly baptized disciples: "Let the one with two coats give to the one who has none. The one who has food should do the same" (3:10f.). In response to both John and Jesus, there appear in Luke's writings some of the church's most memorable and generous characters. For example, only Luke preserves the memory of the wealthy women "who assisted Jesus and the Twelve out of their means" (8:1-3). Only Luke passes on the story of Zacchaeus, the little tax collector and cheater, who literally "jumps out of his tree" with delight to welcome Jesus with the words: "I give half of my belongings to the poor, Lord. If I have defrauded anyone in the least, I pay him back four-fold" (19:8). While this story is preserved by Luke primarily to indicate that Jesus' message of salvation is open to *all people,* even to one from among the despised social class of "tax collector" and "sinner" (19:2, 7), nonetheless, Luke's story also gives his readers an indication of how to respond to that saving message: with joy and generosity!

In the Acts of the Apostles, Luke continues to set before his Christians the challenge to share *whatever they have to give* with the needy. *Barnabas* is held up as a model believer when he sells a farm that he owned and makes a donation of the money, laying it at the apostles' feet (Act 4:36-37). In Acts 16:15ff., *Lydia*, a dealer in purple goods, offers her home as a place of refuge and prayer for Paul and his companions. By way of contrast, *Ananias and Sapphira*, his wife, fall dead at the feet of Peter when they pretend to be generous. Having sold their property, they put aside a part of the proceeds for themselves. The "deadly" consequences of their lack of honesty and generosity show how seriously the early church took Jesus at his word (Acts 5:1-10). Peter also denounces *Simon*, a magician in Samaria, who presumed to try to buy the gift and power of the Holy Spirit.

> Simon, may you and your money rot — thinking that God's gift can be bought. You can have no portion or lot in this affair. Your heart is not steadfastly on God . . . I see you poisoned with gall and caught in the grip of sin. (Acts 8:20f.).

Still other prominent and well-to-do characters in the Acts are held up by Luke as imitable examples of the "generous ones who have" responded to the call of Jesus and to the needs of "those who do not have" in their midst. *Simon*, a leather tanner, offered his home for Peter and others for a considerable time (Acts 9:42). *The whole community at Antioch*, upon hearing of the famine in Jerusalem, was challenged to "set something aside, each according to their means, to send it to the relief of those in Judea" (Acts 11:29). *Paul* commends the pastors of the church at Miletus to help the needy first of all, in this way:

> Never did I set my heart on anyone's silver and gold or envy the way he dressed. You yourselves know that these hands of mine have served both my needs and those of my companions. I have always pointed out to you that it is by such hard work that you must help the weak. You need to recall the words of the Lord Jesus himself, who said, 'There is more happiness in giving than in receiving." (Acts 20:33-35).

Perhaps the most familiar passage concerning the poor and the rich in all the gospels is that of the "rich young man," who approached Jesus to ask: "What must I do to share in everlasting life?" In Luke's version of this encounter, the man is a rich member of the ruling class. He has kept all the commandments since his boyhood. Believers of every age know, almost by heart, Jesus' invitation to follow him, as well as the man's response.

> 'There is one more thing you must do. Sell all you have and give to the poor. You will have treasure in heaven. Then, come and follow me." On hearing this, the man grew melancholy, for he was a very rich man. (18:18-24).

Consider, however, that in Luke's recounting of this well-known passage, one does *not* hear that the man "went away sad" (as he does in Mk 10:22 and in Mt 19:22). Rather, after growing melancholy, the man just seems to drift into the crowd. Luke's omission of this sad departure makes it possible for the reader of his account to imagine the man listening in as Jesus continues: "How hard it will be for the rich to go into the kingdom of God! Indeed, it is easier for a camel to go through a needle's eye than for a rich person to enter the kingdom of heaven" (18:24). Such a message could cause heavy sadness to fall upon any wealthy person's heart. But Jesus' following statement could just as well have lifted the rich ruler from sadness to hope. For Jesus' disciples went on to ask: "Who, then, can be saved?" And Jesus responded; "Things that are impossible for human beings are possible for God" (18:26f.). Along with the rich ruler, who could not act immediately upon Jesus' challenge to sell all he had and give to the poor, today's readers of Luke's gospel can take heart that there is still room, even for people of means, to respond to Jesus and have "treasure in heaven."

The overwhelming evidence is in, and Luke's case stands. For one who is not desperately poor, to be a Lucan Christian is to see the world through Jesus' eyes and to respond generously to what one sees. The world's poor and needy stand before Christian believers. They are the visible presence of the hidden Lord on earth today. If Christians ask "Who are you, sir?" as Paul did on the road to Damascus, they would *not* hear: "I am that Jesus whom you are persecuting" (Acts 26:9-15). They *would hear,* however: "I am that Jesus whom you have the privilege to love and respect in the person of the poor. I am the one who asks you to help me experience my worth as a human being. I am your brother or sister in the inner city, who needs power as well as charity in order to put food on the table for my children. I am the one you care for when you give me support through charitable collections in your church. I am also the one you respect enough to write letters for, on behalf of legislation that will alleviate my situation. Even if you do not have a room for me to sleep in or a job for me to go to each day, whenever you give me your time, your love, and your respect, you are giving yourself to me, Jesus, your Lord and the Lord of the poor."

In Luke's presentation of Jesus' predilection for the poor, as well as in his story of how it is lived out in the primitive church of Acts, the Christian believer of today has an ample and clear enough summons to share whatever she or he has been blessed with, be it home, power, time, or "one of two coats." Moreover, Luke's writings clearly challenge the churches to form a Christian community that includes the poor in a respectful manner. This is a community that would look like the community in the Acts of the Apostles, a community that is attached only to God, one that generously reaches out beyond itself, beyond its own geographical locale or religious, economic, or social boundaries. This is the Christian community that can proudly say to the world: "We are one with the poor, not only in our prayers and charity, but also in our commitment to enable all people to experience their dignity as daughters and sons of God!"

The Message for the Poor

What Luke says to his well-to-do readers *about the poor* is good news *for the poor*: "Be generous and respectful with your needy brothers and sisters, for this is being like Jesus, who brought glad tidings to the poor and stood in solidarity with them." But what is the impact of Luke's message upon the poor themselves, beyond some comfort in knowing that others have been challenged to respect and assist them in their need? Are the poor merely to wait in "this vale of tears" as humble recipients of the gifts of others, until "the reign of God is finally theirs," in heaven (6:20)?

"It is because you are needy," says Luke's Jesus to the poor, "that you are the special object of my Father's concern. My mission on earth was highlighted by a challenge to the 'more comfortable' members of God's people on your behalf. However, you are not special because of the miserable condition in which you find yourselves. Your misery is not what I want. You are special because you are so conscious of your need for someone else besides yourselves in your struggle for happiness and dignity. Take heart! Not one of you is neglected by my Father! So, fear not, little flock. You are loved very much. However, be careful not to be lulled into the trap that so many have fallen into. Namely, 'avoid greed in *all* its forms (12:15). In your desire to become human, also be responsible citizens of God's kingdom on earth, 'growing rich in the sight of God and not for yourselves alone' (12:20). In your radical need, you live from day to day, trying to provide the bare necessities for yourselves and your families. In your basic existence, be assured that 'your Father knows you need such things' (12:30). At the same time, you must 'seek out his kingship over you,' without excessive worry or fear (12:22-31). Thus you, perhaps more than anyone else, can provide for the whole world and church the example of what it means to be committed to the values of the kingdom. By your unfailing love of our Father, your family, and other needy ones, you will amaze everyone! You will show them what it really means to be sons and daughters of the Most High. In your solidarity with God's other needy children, you will provide for all the greatest lesson in Christian living, for you will be the living example of what it means for 'students to be on a par with their teacher' (6:40). You will be 'as compassionate as your Father is compassionate' (6:36). You will be living out the most important of the values of Christianity. For, to be trusting and dedicated Christians, in the midst of your own situation, speaks more clearly than any words that: 'Our treasure and our hearts are in God!" (12:34).

Luke's message to the poor is as challenging as it is to the rich. They will, therefore, also have to pray without ceasing, without losing heart. Their persistent pleas for what they need, however, will be heard: "If you, with all your sins, know how to give your children good things, how much more will your heavenly Father give you the Holy Spirit when you ask him" (11:13). Luke urges the poor never to give up, not until they have experienced the wholeness that is rightfully theirs. They can remember the widow who sought her rights from the unjust judge. Her persistence put the fear of God into the powerful judge of the story: "I care little for God or for man, but this widow is wearing me out. I am going to settle in her favor or she will end by doing me violence" (18:4f.). By responsible, faith-filled, and concrete attempts at "renewing the face of the earth," the poor work hand in hand with a God who wants dignity for all his people. "Will he delay long over you, do you suppose? I tell you, he will give you swift justice" (18:7f.). "Blessed are you poor, indeed," says Luke, "for when you are compassionate, when you reach out to others and not only for yourselves, yours *is* the kingdom of God!"

It is the paradoxical good news of God and Luke that, when those who are poor hear and act upon Jesus' word, they know the fulfillment of the promises made to the rich man! By following Jesus and putting the values of the kingdom before all else, the poor "receive a plentiful return *in this age* and life everlasting in the age to come" (18:30). As the poor strive to come to their deserved place in the Body of Christ, they can relish Jesus' enlivening word:

> Consider the ravens: they do not sow, they do not reap, they have neither cellar nor barn — yet God feeds them. How much

> more important you are than the birds! Which of you by worrying can add a moment to your life span? If the smallest things are beyond your power, why be anxious about the rest? Your Father knows what you need. Seek out his kingship over you. The rest will follow in turn. (12:24-26, 31).

Conclusion: Of Sparrows and Pennies

Chapter 12 of Luke's gospel, which has just been used to sum up his message to the poor, can also serve well as a summary chapter for careful and prayerful meditation on the crucial issues that Christians, both poor and rich, must face. The chapter begins and ends, provocatively enough, with *warnings:* first, against hypocrisy (v. 1), and, in conclusion, against false interpretations of the signs of the times (vv. 54-59). Featured in this "mini-sermon" of Jesus are some of his most revealing *challenges* concerning possessions and detachment from them. "Avoid greed in all its forms. One may be wealthy, but one's possessions do not guarantee life" (v. 15). "Those who store up extra goods in newly built grain bins will lose their lives this very night. That is the way it works with those who grow rich for themselves instead of growing rich in the sight of God" (v. 21). The pervading spirit of the chapter seems to be found in the *motivating refrain,* "Do not be afraid," repeated three times: "Do not be afraid of those who kill the body and can do no more" (v. 4); "Fear nothing. You are worth more than a flock of sparrows" (v. 7); "Do not live in fear, little flock. It has pleased your Father to give you the kingdom" (v. 32).

The cumulative effect of these warnings, challenges, and refrains comes with Jesus' "punch line": "Sell what you have and give alms. Get purses for yourselves that do not wear out, a never-failing treasure with the Lord, which no thief comes near nor any moth destroys. Wherever your treasure lies, there your heart will be!" (vv. 33-35). By his careful arrangement of this chapter, Luke not only alerts his readers to the death-dealing effects of greed, he also gives hope and life to those who really want to be of Jesus' flock. Moreover, inspired by his message "not to fear," Luke's readers can confidently let others know that they, too, are "worth more than a flock of sparrows!" Luke has even concretized the way for his Christians to do this: "Sell what you have and give yourselves away! Then you will be free of the snares of earthly wealth and from attachment to grain bins and failing treasures! Your hearts will then be with God, your only treasure!"

Chapter 12 of Luke's gospel has been chosen as a prayerful way of concluding his treatment of the poor and the rich. It is quite fitting, therefore, that Luke himself concludes this chapter by having Jesus say:

> Tell me, why do you not judge for yourselves what is just. When you are going with your opponent to appear before a magistrate, try to settle with him on the way lest he turn you over to the judge, and the judge deliver you up to the jailer, and the jailer throw you into prison. I warn you, you will not be released from there *until you have paid the last penny.* (vv. 57-59).

Jesus' "last word" in chapter 12, that is, "the last penny," leads his hearers back to the beginning, which is the true "end" of it all: "Are not five sparrows sold for a few pennies? Yet not one of them is neglected by God" (v. 6). As Luke's readers turn to the theme of justice and peace in Luke-Acts, they will see just how true Jesus is to his word.

2

OF JUSTICE AND PEACE

If contemporary Christians, be they well-to-do or poor, can profitably look to Luke for such an enlightening message, it would seem likely that his writings would also be the place to search for clear direction on the relevant issues of justice and peace. And this is indeed the case. For Luke presents Jesus and the early church as vibrant agents of peace in the first Christian century. However, even though the following examination of the text reveals such powerful Lucan statements as Luke 11:42 ("Woe to you Pharisees! You pay tithes on mint and rue, while neglecting *justice* and the love of God") and Acts 10:36 ("This is the message God has sent to the children of Israel, the good news of *peace* proclaimed through Jesus Christ, who is Lord over all"), it is important not to read into the text more than is there. This caution is given because Luke's first century perspective on justice and peace is not quite as "global" (e.g., concern for reordering society in the "first and third worlds") as twentieth century Christians might expect or wish.

The only Greek word that Luke uses for his "good news of *peace*" is *eirene.* While the word occures only 13 times in the gospel and 5 times in the Acts (compared with the many passages in Luke concerning the rich and the poor), the placement of Luke's peace passages is very significant, as we shall see. This term, coming into Greek from the Hebrew, *shalom,* has a full and clear meaning. When one has *shalom* or *eirene,* one is whole, at peace within oneself and with others, in good health, has rest, and lives peaceably with others. From the Greek comes the English name, Irene, which makes me think of the only three women I have known that bear that name. My aunt Irene, who died a few years ago, was a peaceful and light-hearted woman. The other two Irenes I know are women religious, one a fifty year old Daughter of Charity of German descent in the Northeast, the other a twenty five year old Mexican American novice in Southern California. It is very interesting to me that all three of these Irenes, from such diverse backgrounds, have embodied for me the biblical meaning of their name. All three of them stand out in my mind and experience as people who have taken their Christian life very seriously, with undying dedication to family, friends, and the people they serve. At the same time, they have done so with a flavor of being at peace within themselves. Even in times of crisis, they have been models for me and for others of a gentle, yet effective, wholeness and integrity. Luke's writings, like these women named Irene, can be good news for confusing and violent times. As Christians examine the significant peace passages in Luke and Acts, they will feel the irresistible urging of Luke to bring God's kingdom of peace to the earth today.

While Luke uses several terms to express his concern for *justice,* his vision is focused by the tradition he passes on from the Hebrew scriptures. At its root, justice means *being right with God in dealing with one's brothers and sisters.* This is the case not only in Luke, but in the whole Bible. And for all its emphasis on love, the Hebrew and Christian scriptures make it clear that love is meaningless without justice. By their contact with Luke, prophets in today's church and world will find themselves standing tall and walking on "the road less travelled" with the prophets of old, like Isaiah, Amos, and Micah. They will join them in proclaiming: "Put away your misdeeds from before my eyes. Cease doing evil. Learn to do good, and make justice your aim! Redress the wronged, hear the orphan's plea, and defend the widow!" (Is. 1:16-18).

Some Facts about Peace in Luke-Acts

When one lines up the 13 peace passages in the gospel of Luke, it is possible to notice some "clusters" and relationships among them which give clear hints to Luke's meaning of the term. For example, the first three occurrences of *eirene* come in the infancy narrative, in chapters 1 and 2. Then, near the end of the gospel, Luke begins and ends his passion-resurrection account with *eirene*, at 19:38, 19:42, and 24:36. Such "clustering" of the term highlights Luke's attempt to present Jesus as a life-long person of peace.

In the infancy account, Zechariah concludes his prayer of blessing God on the occasion of John's birth in the following way:

> And you, child, shall be called the prophet of the Most High; for you shall go before the Lord to prepare straight paths for him,

> giving his people a knowledge of salvation in freedom from their sins. All this is the work of the kindness of our God; he, the Dayspring, shall visit us in his mercy, to shine on those who sit in darkness and in the shadow of death, to guide our feet into *the way of peace* (1:76-79).

In just this one passage, today's Christian can note the emphasis Luke places on peace. It is the "last word" of Zechariah's prayer, both in the Greek and in English. Something of the term's special meaning can also be seen from its association with the prayer's hope for "straight paths of salvation and freedom from sin" and "the kindness and mercy of God for those who sit in darkness." Then, when the angels praise God ("Glory to God in high heaven and *peace* on earth to those on whom his favor rests," 2:14) and when Simeon blesses God ("Now, master, you can dismiss your servant *in peace;* you have fulfilled your word," 2:29), it becomes clear for whom God's peace is meant: it is meant for everyone! So be alert, readers of Luke's gospel! The Lord wants to bestow his peaceful favor on common Jewish shepherds and on pious temple people alike. His peace means freedom from fear and an invitation to come to him (2:8-17). Those for whom his peace is meant are both Jew and non-Jew, because all the peoples have been favored by the saving light of God, incarnate in the child Jesus (2:30-32).

To begin Jesus' life with the proclamation of peace is not enough for Luke. He also ends his account of Jesus' mission on earth, making *eirene* the "last word." In the triumphal entry into Jerusalem, Luke is the only evangelist to add a significant phrase: "Blest be he who comes as king in the name of the Lord! *Peace in heaven and glory in the highest!*" (19:38). This additional proclamation of peace echoes the angels' announcement to the shepherds (in 2:14). Moreover, only Luke follows the entry into Jerusalem with the poignant scene that finds Jesus weeping over Jerusalem and saying: "If only you had known *the path to peace* this day; but you have completely lost it from view!" (19:42). Jesus is the path to peace promised by Zechariah (in 1:79). His life and teachings of peace should have led all to peace. Instead, some people try to thwart Jesus and his disciples in their liberating mission:

> Some of the Pharisees in the crowd said to him, 'Teacher, rebuke your disciples (for proclaiming you as king of peace).' He replied, 'If they were to keep silence, I tell you the very stones would cry out." (19:39-40)

In fact, continues Luke, some people will even put Jesus to death in order to establish their own brand of "peace." For them, peace is wrongly a *status-quo* acceptance of traditional religious teachings and political leadership. Not so for Jesus! For him, peace is "proclaiming liberty to the captives" (4:18). For him, the mission of peace is so central that it must be carried on even at the risk of being seen as one "who stirs up the people" (see trial accusations, at 23:1-6). Yet, any seeker of truth will conclude, as Pilate himself did, that they "had no charge against him arising from their allegations" (23:14). Jesus and other peacemakers will not walk a smooth path. But even though the path leads to death, it is a path of freedom, light, and *eirene*.

Luke ends his gospel with the comforting words to his disciples: "Peace to you" (24:36). Just as the fear-filled shepherds were calmed and filled with joy by the angel's announcement of his birth, so now the trembling disciples are uplifted and encouraged by Jesus' own message of peace after his death and resurrection. In this way, Luke sums up Jesus' whole life and mission by his last words, which are the fulfillment of Zechariah's prayer and promise. John's father had prayed that John would prepare the way for the one who would "give people a knowledge of salvation in freedom from their sins" (1:77). Jesus leaves his disciples, in 24:46-49, with these words:

> Thus it is written that the Messiah must suffer and rise from the dead on the third day. In his name, penance for the remission of sin is to be preached to all nations, beginning at Jerusalem. You are witnesses of this. See, I send down upon you the promise of my Father. Remain here in the city until you are clothed with *power from on high.*

That "power from on high" would, of course, be the Holy Spirit (Acts 2). It would also be a *power for peace,* enabling the church in time to take up and complete Jesus' own mission on earth. By a survey of the remaining passages concerning peace in the gospel and Acts, today's disciple of Luke's Jesus can discover some concrete directions for their peace efforts in the world.

Lighting a Fire on the Earth

> I have come to light a fire on the earth. How I wish the blaze were ignited! I have a baptism to receive. What anguish I feel till it is over! Do you think I have come to establish *peace* on the earth? I assure you, the contrary is true; I have come for division. From now on, a household of five will be divided, three against two and two against three; father will be split against son and son against father, mother against daughter and daughter against

> mother, mother-in-law against daughter-in-law and daughter-in-law against mother-in-law. (12:49-53)

There is no way to get around it! In both Luke's and Matthew's gospels, Jesus says he has come "not to establish peace but division." This startling saying stands out as a passage of contradiction. How contrary to the Christian community's perception of Jesus! He himself proclaims that he has come to light a fire on earth that will pit loved ones against one another rather than bring them together! The anguish and confusion (and embarrassment!) which Christian readers feel upon encountering this passage makes them pause to ask: what does he mean, and how can this be? It is also very important for them to try to discover the source of the anguish Jesus feels "until it is over!"

What did Luke's Jesus mean to say here to his first century Christian community of faith? What is God saying in this passage about the mission of peace to his people today? It is helpful to look at the parables which immediately precede this key text. The first concerns those who await their master's return from a wedding (12:35-40). The second is the parable of the far-sighted steward (12:42-48). It becomes evident that any faithful follower of Jesus will encounter painful conflicts and division. Therefore, *to be ready,* to be a disciple of true peace, a follower of Jesus cannot expect that their journey will be untroubled and "peaceful." Jesus' mission will involve much misunderstanding and being misunderstood, even by one's own family. In fact, the Christian gospel of peace charges its hearers to a whole new and much broader understanding of family and kinship. "My mother, my brothers and sisters, are those who hear the word of God and act upon it" (8:21). That word also calls for far more than ordinary human peace, well-being, or "freedom from troubles." Being involved in the establishment of God's true peace on earth led Jesus to a "baptism of fire," that is, to his death. It will also lead those who follow him to many "deaths." They will have to clarify their traditional and received values *in the light of his cross:* "What profit does one show who gains the whole world and destroys oneself in the process?" (9:25). Jesus' life and message led him and his first followers to trial and confrontation with religious and political earthly leaders: "Pilate, this Jesus stirs up the people by his teachings. Crucify him" (23:5); "Roman commander, kill this Paul! Rid the earth of the likes of him! He isn't worthy to live!" (Acts 22:22). Disciples of Jesus will have to be prepared for the same divisive struggles that Jesus and Paul encountered, even with family and fellow "church members." "And if anyone is ashamed of me and of my doctrines, the Son of Man will be ashamed of them when he comes in his glory and in the glory of his father and his holy angels" (9:26).

Indeed, if twentieth century Christians accept the challenging peace mission of their Lord, they, like him, will know anguish, "until it is over." They will follow him by proclaiming and bringing liberty to captives and recovery of sight to the blind. They will do whatever is in their power to bring those who weep to laughter and those who are poor to satisfying consolation and respect. But how does one do more than *say* "*peace* to this house," as Jesus recommends to his disciples in 10:5-6? How can today's followers of Jesus be effective peace makers?

Fulfilling the Mission of Peace: Doing Justice

"If you want peace, work for justice." This statement of Pope Paul VI has become the rallying call of the post-Vatican II church. Luke concretizes this modern challenge in his writings by saying: "If you want the peace of the kingdom, hear and imitate Jesus as he boldly confronts the leaders of his day: 'Woe to you, scribes and pharisees. You pay tithes on mint and rue and all the garden plants, while neglecting justice and the love of God' (11:42). *Watch Jesus* put his words into action as he forgives the despised sinner woman before sending her off "in peace" (7:50). *Then, you do likewise* with those who are despised in your community, those who are seen as unworthy of respect. When you go to worship on Sunday, beware that you do not perform empty worship, 'reciting prayers to keep up appearances, while really going through the savings of widows' (12:45-47). Instead, honor the one who has no honor. Give hope to the one who has no hope. *See Jesus* care in a special way for the woman with the twelve-year hemorrhaging problem, 'incurable at any doctor's hands' (8:43), before he sends her off 'in peace' (8:48). *Do likewise* with those who are despairing because of long illness or sadness. Comfort them with your healing word and visits. You may be 'just what the doctor ordered.' Even though you cannot take away the physical illness, you may lighten the burden with your peaceful love and respect."

The message of Luke's Jesus carries on the pervasive challenge of the prophets concerning justice. To be holy is not a matter of individual piety or of appearances. It is the levelling of class distinctions before God, who cares especially for widows, orphans, and strangers, so as to raise them to their dignity as his daughters and sons. Through Mary's prayer, Luke says; "He has deposed the mighty from their thrones and has raised the lowly to high places. The hungry he has given every good thing, while the rich he has sent empty away" (1:52-53). This hopeful yearning of Luke's Mary is like an echo of Isaiah's cry:

> Build up, build up, prepare the way; remove the stumbling blocks from my people's path . . . On high I dwell, and in holiness, and with the crushed and dejected in spirit, to revive the spirits of the dejected, to revive the hearts of the crushed . . . The type of fasting I wish is this: releasing those bound unjustly, untying every yoke; sharing your bread with the hungry, sheltering the oppressed and the homeless; clothing the naked when you see them, and not turning your back on your own. Then your light shall break forth like the dawn, and your wound shall quickly be healed. (Isaiah 57:14-16 and 58:6-8)

The lowly and unprotected ones are thus seen as the special concern of God, Isaiah and Luke.

God Gives Swift Justice through His Ministers

At the end of Jesus' parable of the corrupt judge and the widow seeking her rights against her opponent, there is an encouraging promise and a challenging warning for all of Luke's readers: "I tell you, God will give swift justice to those who call out to him day and night. But when the Son of Man comes, will he find any faith on the earth?" (18:7-8). Such a promise-warning bore fruit in the early church of the Acts, when prayerful discernment led the Twelve to action on behalf of the Greek widows "who were being neglected in the daily distribution of food, as compared with the widows of those who spoke Hebrew" (Acts 6:1). While Luke does not specifically address the problems of justice in the same "global" terms as the church does today, the roots of the contemporary Christian justice mission in the "third and fourth worlds" are clearly seen in Luke's efforts to enlighten the social consciousness of his readers. In this case of the Greek widows, it is a matter of language and cultural discrimination that Luke addresses. In the previous section of this book, he confronted the economic status question by challenging both rich and poor to search for their treasure in God and in the values of Jesus. In chapters to follow, we shall see how Luke addresses other modes of oppression and discrimination which he saw operative in his community of faith (e.g., see chapters on "Women and Men" and "Gospel of Forgiveness"). Indeed, the kingdom of God is for everyone.

To put on a Lucan spirituality that pays strict attention to the love of God and fellow humans under the banner of justice and peace, Christians today are invited to hard and soul-searching work. They are challenged by Luke to evaluate their own prejudices and to respond to the prejudices that abound in the world around them, near and far. Once having meditated on the needs of the underprivileged and unjustly deprived ones of their world, Luke's readers will be responsive after the manner of Mary, Jesus, and the characters of the early church community. Like Mary they will pray that God "will raise up the lowly and put down the mighty" (1:52). Like Jesus, they will challenge the world today: "When you see a cloud rising in the West, you say that rain is coming — and so it does. When the wind blows from the South, you say it is going to be hot — and so it is. You hypocrites! If you can interpret the portents of earth and sky, why can you not interpret the present time? Tell me, why do you not judge for yourselves what is just?" (12:54-57). Like the joyful Zacchaeus, they will stand their ground in the midst of murmuring and "give half their belongings to the poor and pay back four-fold anyone they have defrauded" (19:8). Like the poor widow (in 21:1-4), they will "give what they cannot afford," be it two copper coins or the time and effort necessary to alleviate the burden of the helpless. Like the outsider Cornelius (in Acts 10:36), they will "fear the Lord" in an effective way, and like Cornelius, teach their whole households to be prayerful and generous.

Earlier in this chapter, it was emphasized how Luke's Jesus felt a "great anguish" because he knew his radical mission of justice and peace would not seem to bring peace at all, but would even cause division (12:49ff.). Luke saw injustice and inequality in his first century community, and knew that his readers (then and now) would share Jesus' anguish "until it was over."

Christians who thirst for justice and peace share Jesus' anguish, and also his vision: "We know our Master's wishes. When much has been given to us, much will be required of us. More will be asked of us to whom more has been entrusted" (12:47-48). They also share his Holy Spirit, which helps them determine the signs of the times. Jesus' mission of justice and peace calls forth prophets from the Christian community of every age. The passionate response that Luke's Jesus elicits is like a "double-edged sword" that includes concrete involvement with victims and perpetrators of all forms of social sin, as well as a deep confidence that the Lord of justice is also involved! Therefore, justice-and-peacemakers can hear in Luke's message the reflection of God's challenge through the prophets, Amos and Isaiah:

> Hear this, you who trample upon the needy and destroy the poor of the land! 'When will the new moon be over, that we may sell our grain, and the sabbath, that we may display the wheat? We will diminish the ephah, add to the shekel, and fix our scales for cheating! We will buy the lowly man for silver, and the poor man for a pair of sandals; even the refuse of the wheat we will sell!'
>
> The Lord has sworn by the pride of Jacob; never will I forget a thing they have done! (Amos 8:4-7).

> Because you reject my word, and put your trust in what is crooked and devious, and depend on it, this guilt of yours shall be like a descending rift, bulging out in a high wall, whose crash comes suddenly, in an instant. It crashes like a potter's jar smashed beyond rescue, and among its fragments cannot be found a shard to scoop fire from the hearth or dip water from the cistern.
>
> For thus said the Lord God, the Holy One of Israel: by waiting and by calm you shall be saved, in quiet and in trust your strength lies . . . The Lord is waiting to show you favor, and he rises to pity you; *for the Lord is a God of justice; blessed are all who wait for him!* (Is 30:12-15 & 18).

Responding wholeheartedly to the God of justice, the God of Amos, Isaiah, and Luke, this is what it means to spread "the good news of peace, proclaimed through Jesus Christ, who is Lord of all!" (Acts 10:37).

3

OF WOMEN AND MEN

In this age of the church and world, with all its serious discussion and anguish over human rights, Luke's writings give a great deal of clear and much needed direction to all people of faith. This is especially true regarding the highly charged issue of women's rights. In his presentation of Jesus as one who treated both women and men with reverence and respect, Luke is straightforward, forceful, and remarkably "enlightened" for his time. As he describes Jesus' life and the beginnings of the early church, he invites readers of both the first and twentieth centuries to interact responsibly with his challenging message, which might best be summed up this way: women and men stand together and side-by-side as equals before God; they are equal in honor and grace, and are blessed with the same gifts and with the same responsibilities as Christian persons in their relationships with God, with each other, and with the world around them. In the pages that follow, each male and female Christian who takes God's word according to Luke seriously will discover a source of light and strength to help them on their journey with their Lord.

The first section of this chapter is intended to organize the myriad of "specifically Lucan" passages which reflect how men and women responded to Jesus. This survey will present to Luke's readers today the opportunity to sharpen their own responses to Jesus as Christian men and women in their own age, society, and church. The second part of the chapter will highlight Luke's special treatment of *the woman,* Mary, attempting to bring out how the Christian community is called to identify with her today. Finally, a brief discussion of the masculine and feminine characteristics of "every person," be that person male or female, is intended to assist readers of Luke to deepen their living encounter with God's word, speaking from within the inmost center of their being.

Women and Men: Side by Side

"There were some women with Jesus, who had been cured of evil spirits and maladies; they were assisting him and the Twelve out of their means" (8:1-3). A thoughtful twentieth-century reader of this passage from Luke's gospel could well pause and say: "Ah! Now I know where the stereotype of women in the church and in society comes from! Look at this! Some *sick* women, who also are *wealthy,* are presented as *assisting* Jesus and his Twelve *male* disciples! Is this what the gospels offer women as hope for equality in our contemporary world?" However, once Luke's gospel and Acts have been examined carefully, one might respond quite differently. For in Luke's two-volume work, women are presented in a favorable light. They are the one's who listen attentively to Jesus' message and respond to it as his truest friends! They are there, standing faithfully at the cross, when the crowd goes home: "All his friends and the women who had accompanied him from Galilee were standing at a distance, watching everything" (23:49). They are the ones who came to the tomb at dawn on the first day of the week to bring spices for Jesus' body (24:1). They are the ones who found the tomb empty and were the first to hear and share the good news of his resurrection (24:5-9). And while they were *not* treated with respect ("the story seemed like nonsense and the Eleven refused to believe them" 24:11), nonetheless, their report got Peter running to the tomb (24:12). Luke presents the women at the tomb as "believers." He leaves his readers with the impression that the male disciples needed much more to get them to believe: "Peter went away full of amazement at what had occurred," (24:12). The women believed without seeing. They believed the word of the two men "in dazzling garments" at the empty tomb. The men believed only after they had seen the risen Jesus. "The Lord has been raised! It is true! He has appeared to Simon!" (24:34). We turn now to examine more fully the faith response of women and men in Luke-Acts.

All four of the gospels reflect Jesus' care for the sick, many of whom were women. In Luke's gospel, Jesus seems to be surrounded by women. Martha and Mary (10:38-42), Joanna, Mary of Magdala, Susanna, and other women responded to Jesus and his needs "out of their means" (8:1-3). These women and many others became more than recipients of Jesus' mercy. They are *bearers of a special message* regarding women in the church and in society. Moreover, by Luke's arrangement of the various accounts that involve women, he poses attitudinal challenges and critical questions to Christians like no other gospel writer does. First, we will look at some obvious Lucan passages that bring out Luke's thrust.

In the first chapter of his gospel, Luke "pairs off" and contrasts the elderly Zechariah, father-to-be of John, with the young maiden Mary, mother-to-be of Jesus. While Zechariah hesitates in doubt at hearing the angel's good news, Mary permits the creative message of God to take life within her. Both the man and the woman were afraid upon receiving the angel's message. The woman, however, said "yes" and gave life! Later in the infancy narrative, Anna is presented as an outstanding example of what it means to be a faithful Israelite. She "gave thanks to God and talked about the child Jesus, to all who looked forward to the deliverance of Jerusalem" (2:38). Although Simeon, who was the first "temple person" to welcome Jesus and his family at the time of the presentation (2:25-35), is also the faithful recipient of God's "saving deed," this could be expected. But for a woman to be singled out as a proclaimer of salvation! Luke has set a tone for his whole two-volume work!

Among Jesus' first words are these; "To no one in Israel was the prophet Elijah sent, but to a widow of Zarephath. Recall, too, the many lepers in Israel in the time of Elisha; yet not one was cured except Naaman the Syrian" (4:26-27). Luke lets his readers know that a foreign man, Naaman, and a foreign woman, the widow, were the recipients of God's favor in the time of the prophets. Thus, when Luke reports Jesus as first doing his saving work (in 4:33-39), it is not surprising that his favor comes to rest on both a man, the one possessed by a demon, and a woman, Simon's mother-in-law, who had been "in the grip of a severe fever." Other "pairs" of Jesus' healing encounters with men and women include those in chapters 7 and 8. A centurion gets Jesus to heal his servant (7:1-10) and then Jesus raises to life the only son of a widowed mother at Naim (7:11-17); a chief of the synagogue requests Jesus' help for his dying daughter, and Jesus not only raises her from the dead (8:40-42, 49-56) but also pauses on his life-giving way to cure the woman suffering from the "incurable" hemorrhage (8:42-48). Such "pairing" dramatically drives home Luke's conviction that women and men are both to be held in generous respect by anyone who dares to be called "Christian." More dramatically still, when one encounters the "centerpiece" of these chapters (in 7:36-50, Luke preserves the story of Jesus' meeting the sinner woman at the home of Simon, the Pharisee), one can almost feel Luke's manner of overturning society's way of dealing with women and sinners.

In the story of "the sinner woman and sinless Simon" occurs the most striking contrast between the way men and women respond to Jesus in the gospel of Luke. The respectable host, Simon, did not welcome Jesus with any of the touching respect that the sinner woman did. In fact, after she had washed his feet with her tears, dried them with her hair, and perfumed and kissed them, the Pharisee is reported to say to himself: "If this man were a prophet, he would know who and what sort of woman this is that touches him — that she is a sinner!" (7:39). Jesus responds to Simon's reproachful attitude with a parable about two men who were forgiven their debts by their master, in 7:41-42. However, the woman, by her signs of loving respect, is a parable in action. So Jesus asks Simon:

> You see this woman? I came to your home and you provided me with no water for my feet. She has washed my feet with her tears and wiped them with her hair. You gave me no kiss, but

> she has not ceased kissing my feet since I entered. I tell you, her many sins are forgiven. Her great love shows this. The one who is forgiven little loves little. (7:44 & 47 translation by M. Zerwick, adapted; see below, p. 126.)

When Jesus tells the woman to go in peace, he is also saying to all of Luke's readers: "Learn a lesson from the woman. Learn a lesson from that part of you which is open and responsive to the love of the Lord. What a lesson to learn! What joy to feel as free and as fully human as this woman in her approach to Jesus! What relief and unbounded joy to hear his final words: "Your faith has been your salvation. Now go in peace" (7:50)! What a sharp challenge to hear: "You see this woman? Have you been as humble and grateful as she?"

Although the account of Peter's denial of Jesus in the courtyard, at the time of Jesus' passion, is found in all four gospels, the following Lucan passage stands out in bold relief:

> They led Jesus away under arrest and brought him to the house of the high priest, while Peter followed at a distance. Later they lighted a fire in the middle of the courtyard and were sitting beside it, and Peter sat among them. A servant girl saw him sitting in the light of the fire. She gazed at him intently, then said: 'This man was with him.' He denied the fact, saying, 'Woman, I do not know him.' (22:54-57).

In the overall picture of his gospel and Acts, Luke might very well be pointing the finger at all of today's church and society and be saying: "Learn from the woman what it is to know Jesus!"

A look at the remaining "man-woman" passages in Luke-Acts will only shed more light on: 1) how insistent Luke's Jesus and the early church were on the equal dignity due to woman and man, and 2) how woman often "does it better" (i.e., responds more readily to Jesus) than her male counterpart.

For example, in chapter 10, the good Samaritan parable highlights the active response of one man who has heard God's word ("You shall love the Lord your God with your whole heart, soul, strength, and mind, and your neighbor as yourself," 10:27), and as a result crosses cultural and religious boundaries to act on behalf of his "half dead neighbor" (10:25-37). Immediately following, in chapter 11, one finds the story of Martha and Mary, in which the anxious "guest master" Martha is told to learn from her sister Mary that "Christian *action follows* Christian *being and listening*." That is, being with Jesus as an active listener is "the better portion" (11:38-42). Side by side, Mary and the good Samaritan show the church its need for attentive listening and spontaneous compassion, not worry and anxious care for "all to be appropriate and in order."

In chapters 13 and 14, within a few verses of each other, Luke's Jesus heals both a badly stooped woman (13:10-13) and a man who suffered from dropsy (14:1-6). Both cures occur on the sabbath. Both result in self-righteous indignation among the chiefs of the synagogue. Both stories end with the same penetrating statement of Jesus:

> You hypocrites! Which of you does not let his ox or ass out of the stall (or pit) on the sabbath to water (or to rescue) it? Should not this daughter of Abraham (or this sick man) be released from her (or his) shackles on the sabbath? (13:15-16 & 14:5).

Both woman and man are worth more than any ox or ass,

which could be cared for on the sabbath. But only Luke, of the four evangelists, has the story of the stooped woman to parallel the miracle account of the man with dropsy. Thus Luke's choice of presenting this "parallel healing account" and the imagery he uses, namely, that she "immediately stood up straight after eighteen years of being drained of strength, quite incapable of standing erect" (vv. 11-13), could be particularly symbolic both for Luke's first audience and for today. Might not such a powerful image be Luke's way of saying that the kingdom of God resembles man and woman, standing tall and side by side, with equal dignity and worth? It would seem so, because he follows these stories with two parables which say that the kingdom of God does resemble: 1) the mustard seed which *a man* plants and 2) the yeast which *a woman* kneads into three measures of flour (13:18 & 21a). Both men and women need to hear the same message: that the kingdom of God is tiny, yet it grows and becomes like the largest of shrubs or like a whole mass of rising dough (13:19 & 21b). Both man and woman also have a significant part to play in bringing the kingdom to its fulness. Another "gospel pair" of man and woman parables reveals a key element of that fulness, namely, the heartfelt repentance and joy experienced when "a shepherd finds the one lost sheep" (15:1-7) or when "the woman retrieves the one silver piece that she had lost" (15:8-10). Indeed, there is untold joy in heaven when a man *or* a woman participates in the reconciliation of a single lost sinner. And when a lost man or woman has been found, "there will be more joy in heaven than over ninety-nine righteous people who have no need to repent" (15:7).

In his Acts of the apostles Luke stresses that it was a church of men and women that gathered in prayer to prepare for the Pentecost coming of the Holy Spirit (Acts 1:14). Both Aeneas, the paralytic male, and Tabitha, the deceased "woman convert," are given life in Jesus' name (Acts 9:32-42). Lydia, as well as the Philippian jailer (in Acts 16) both provide imitable examples of what it means to put new-born faith to the effective service of their fellow Christians. And finally in Acts 17:34, both Dionysius and Damaris, influential male and female members of the Athens community, became believers upon hearing Paul, while many others "sneered at the good news of the risen Jesus."

In the final chapters of his gospel, Luke has gathered together several examples that might provoke more questioning for today's society and church than they did in the first century. Can one detect a certain prejudice in favor of woman here? Is woman really more ready and capable to respond to Jesus and to God's word? It would seem so from the stark contrast between the widow woman who entrusted her life into God's hands by giving her last two coins, indeed, "every penny she had to live on" (21:1-4) and the scribes who put ritual piety ahead of mercy toward the needy (20:45-47). Even on the way of the cross, while Simon of Cyrene was forced to help Jesus carry his cross (23:26), the daughters of Jerusalem openly wept and exposed themselves as believers along the way (23:27-31). Likewise, while both men and women are present at the time of Jesus' death and resurrection, Luke's female characters seem to be hopeful and believing, while the male disciples, with the exception of Joseph of Arimathea, are portrayed as helpless and close to despair (23:49-24:12). Is Luke really saying that "nobody does it better" than the woman?

Nobody Does It Better: Mary and the Church in Luke-Acts

There is so much "Mary material" in Luke's gospel that many people have concluded that Luke must have known Mary personally and then written about her from this association. Whether or not Luke knew her (and many biblical scholars do not think that he had to know her to present his gospel as he does), it is obvious that Luke wants his readers to know *how well Mary knew Jesus!* "Like mother like son," the saying goes. For Luke, the opposite is also true: "Like the son, so the mother." Notice how Mary's deep trust in God overcomes her fear when she receives the word of God from the angel (1:28-38). Jesus would later "teach her" even more about his and her role, namely, that they both "had to be about his father's business" (2:49; see also Jesus' acceptance of his Father's will in the garden of Gethsemane, at 22:42). See Mary in the crowds, in the two other places where Luke mentions her explicitly in his gospel, as she hears again the meaning of her role as mother: "Blest is the one who hears God's word and acts upon it" (8:21 and 11:28). In fact, the son and the mother learned from each other. And it is in imitation of them both that Luke's readers will put on their intense dedication to God's will, "treasuring all these things in their hearts" (2:19; 2:51, and Acts 1:14).

From Imitation to Identification

Many people refer to the gospel of Luke as "the gospel of Mary." This title is appropriate only if the title is understood in a certain sense. For the gospel of Luke is *not* a gospel *about* Mary. It is not even primarily a gospel about imitation of Mary. Rather, Luke asks the church of his day and ours to *see in Mary what it, the church, has become,* through the gospel event of Jesus! Mary is, for Luke, the personified challenge for his church to enter a process of identification with her. This subtle but very significant difference between "the church imitating Mary" and "the church becoming itself" is made even clearer when Christians see the inner weavings of the Mary-church fabric throughout Luke's gospel and Acts. Mary, indeed, *is* the historical mother of Jesus. As a virgin maiden, she did consent to "conceive and bear a son by the Holy Spirit and the power of the Most High" (1:31 and 35). However, in Luke's vision, Mary is foremost the fulfillment of God's promises to his whole people through the prophets. She is Israel, "the highly favored Daughter of Zion," as the angel addresses her (1:28). She is the ideal representative of the whole people of God, the church, and therefore, she and the church can appropriate to themselves the promises of Zechariah, the prophet: "Rejoice heartily, O Daughter Zion! Shout for joy, O Daughter Jerusalem! See, your king shall come to you; a Saviour is he, meek, and riding on an ass, on a colt, the foal of an ass" (Zech 9:9). Luke wants his people to rejoice also in the message of the prophet, Zephaniah, intended for and fulfilled in Mary and in the church:

> Shout for joy, O Daughter Zion! Sing joyfully, O Israel! The Lord has removed the judgement against you; he has turned away your enemies; the king of Israel, the Lord, is *in your midst;* you have no further misfortune to fear. On that day, it shall be said to Jerusalem: 'Fear not, O Zion, be not discouraged. The Lord is in your midst, a mighty saviour. He will rejoice over you

> with gladness, and renew you in his love; he will sing joyfully because of you, as one sings at festivals.' (Zeph. 3:14-17).

In other words, Luke is saying: *Mary is you, the church* born of Jesus' death and resurrection! You, church, are the new people of Israel, the highly favored one, with the Lord *in your midst* by the power of the Holy Spirit! You, church, like Mary, are also the "new ark of the covenant." For just as the Spirit of God came upon the ark of the covenant (Exodus 40:35), so did the Holy Spirit overshadow Mary (Luke 1:35), and so does it guide you on your journey, in the twentieth century.

By identifying Mary and the church, as he does, Luke makes it possible and correct for the church to pray the Magnificat as its own prayer: "For God has made us his own servants, looking on us and our lowliness. He has showered his mercy on us who fear him, so that we indeed are called blest" (1:48; see also Malachi 3:11). Luke also asks the church to realize its dignity: "Blest are we among all people" (1:42; see also Judith 3:18f.). The living Daughter of Zion is the church, being asked to "treasure all these things," to reflect on them on her prayerful journey (2:19), and to act upon the Word of God she bears within her heart (8:21)! Luke's gospel is indeed "the gospel of the church," identifying itself with Mary. And it truly can be said: "Nobody does it better!"

Of Anima and Animus

Luke's emphasis on Mary, the church, and man-woman, can assist twentieth century Christians in their encounters with their deepest inner selves. Many maturing Christians today are looking for help with their inner search for wholeness and personal integrity. They can learn much from what Luke has presented in his writings.

As those learned in contemporary psychology are eager to point out, every individual person has within them both masculine and feminine components which help guide and direct their "outer lives." The masculine elements are sometimes described as strength, clarity, and objectivity. In both men and women, this component, called the *animus*, enables the Christian pilgrim to be strong and steady without being rigid. Its clarity gives light and a welcome vision in what might seem to be hazy or obscure times. Its objectivity enables one to focus on life and its issues without becoming too emotionally entangled. Just so, in every woman and man, one's feminine inner partner, called the *anima*, is characterized as gentle, intuitive, and receptive. These *anima* characteristics move each person, whether male or female, toward activities which are patient, kind, and peaceful. Reverence and deep care are marks of the *anima*. Its intuitive inner eye goes "to the heart of the matter" and understands it, even when words cannot express it. Its receptivity allows oneself and others to enter freely and with welcome, providing space and reassurance for further growth. Once Christian pilgrims acknowledge that *all* these dynamics are present within them, and once they determine which are dominant and which are less developed, they can take more charge of their whole lives and self direction. They can also reap the benefits of Luke's insights for this "inner part" of their spiritual journey. Indeed, it is possible to see in his writings the attempt of a first century male to develop that side of Christian self-consciousness that is called *anima*, the feminine. Even if he did not choose to do so intentionally, Luke nevertheless reveals in his writings a great sensitivity to the needed balance of *anima* gentleness and *animus* strength, of *anima* intuition and *animus* clarity, of *anima* receptivity and *animus* objectivity. He communicates this sensitivity by favoring the *anima* side of the balance.

Luke's "Balanced Approach" to Life and God: Today

From what has been discovered in Luke-Acts, one might conclude that Luke thought women were better than men in their way of responding to God. Perhaps such a corrective could be helpful in the world and church, even today. However, it seems that there would be no "lasting value" in such a conclusion. In fact, the result of such a reading of Luke might only serve to promote a new imbalance among God's people, a new inequality, namely, that "we now have a new 'better half.'" The more salutary value and challenge of Luke's treatment of men and women for today lies in the call for all the members of the church, both men and women, to integrate their feminine sides (their gentleness, receptivity, and intuitive nature) more fully into their Christian personalities. As a consequence, the church could truly become the "living Ark of the Spirit" that "does it best."

A further possible means of putting on Luke's spirituality in this regard concerns one's prayer and Luke's vision of God. If both women and men were to take the risk to envision the feminine side of God, and if they were to let themselves know and be known by a God who is just as accepting and forgiving as she/he is strong and challenging, they might well discover new depths in this most intimate relationship of their Christian lives.

4

GOOD NEWS OF GOD'S FORGIVENESS

One year after the nearly critical attempt on his life in 1983, Pope John Paul II was featured on a TIME magazine cover, visiting his would be assassin, Mehmet Ali Agca. Superimposed on this cover picture were the words: "Why forgive?" By his compassionate look, the Pope was answering that question. He was telling the whole world that the healing forgiveness of Jesus was still desperately needed in its midst. By his hand clasp of pardon, he was imitating Jesus, who forgave those who had crucified him: "Father, forgive them for they know not what they do" (23:34). Jesus' words of mercy from the cross, according to Luke, seemed to have inspired one of the two thieves crucified with him to say to the other:

> We deserve this death sentence. We are only paying the price for what we have done, but this man has done nothing wrong . . . Jesus, remember me when you enter upon your reign. (And Jesus replied:) I assure you, this day you shall be with me in paradise (23:41-43).

Jesus' forgiveness from the cross had a healing effect, says Luke, not only on those present, but also on his church. This is vividly expressed in Acts when Stephen, at the moment before his martyrdom, cried out: "Lord, do not hold this sin against them" (Acts 7:63). Why forgive? Was not the hard heart of Saul, "who concurred in the act of killing and in the harrassment of the church" (Acts 8:1), softened by Stephen's imitation of Jesus' forgiveness? Did not Stephen's example of pardon prepare Saul to understand better Jesus' words on the road to Damascus: "I am Jesus whom you are persecuting" (Acts 9:5)? In a very real way, Stephen's forgiveness in his dying could be said to have paved the way for *Saul* to become *Paul,* the apostle of reconciliation to both Jew and Gentile. In his dramatic visit to forgive Agca, Pope John Paul II was carrying on the healing tradition rooted in the gospel and Acts of Luke. Followers of Jesus know the answer to TIME's question: They forgive because they want to bring all people, even their enemies, into God's reign.

There are more than thirty passages in Luke-Acts which feature the mercy and pardon of God. This great number of "forgiveness stories" alone makes it clear to his readers that compassion and pardon are to be an integral part of their spiritual journey with Jesus. Why forgive? Certainly because such forgiveness can draw others to God. Even more basically, because God has forgiven us first! "Be compassionate as your Father is compassionate," says Luke's Jesus at the end of his sermon on the plain (6:36). By journeying with Jesus through the merciful pages of Luke's gospel and Acts, Christians will be schooled in what reconciliation with God and others is really about. Then, by a careful examination of three passages, they will see: 1) that *God* is the one who *initiates any pardon or forgiveness*; and 2) *how they should feel and respond* in the presence of such a compassionate God. Thus they will be challenged to move from a stance of guilt and fear of God ("Lord, I am an unworthy person") to enter confidently into a warm relationship with the Lord who "has come not to invite the self-righteous to a change of heart, but sinners" (5:32).

Preparing the Way for God's Mercy

In the entire gospel tradition, John the Baptist is known as "the precursor" of Jesus, the forerunner, "who would make ready the way of the Lord" (3:4; Mt 3:3; Mk 1:3; Jn 1:23). It is Luke alone, however, who includes the following detailed description of John's role as the herald of God's mercy and forgiveness:

> He (John) will never drink wine or strong drink, and he will be filled with the Holy Spirit from his mother's womb. Many of the children of Israel will he bring back to the Lord, their God. God himself will go before him, in the spirit and power of Elijah, to turn the hearts of fathers to their children, and the rebellious to the wisdom of the just, and to prepare for the Lord a people well-disposed. (1:15-17)

Indeed, prays John's father, Zechariah (at 1:76-77): "You, o child, shall be called the prophet of the most high. You shall prepare straight paths for the Lord, giving his people a knowledge of salvation, in freedom from their sins." And so John did! "He went about the entire region of the Jordan, proclaiming a baptism of repentance which led to the forgiveness of sins" (3:3).

Mary is another forerunner and herald of God's merciful favor on his people. In her Magnificat prayer, she sets the stage for Jesus' coming by saying:

> God's mercy is from age to age on those who fear him . . . He has upheld Israel his servant, ever mindful of his mercy; even as he promised our fathers, promised Abraham and his descendants forever (1:50 & 54f.).

Of all the evangelists, only Luke goes to such lengths to make it clear to his Christian community that Jesus would begin his earthly life and ministry in a setting so rich in God's promises of mercy! The Lucan stage was indeed set for the greatest act of reconciliation ever to be performed on this earth!

Following through on God's Mercy: In the Acts

This chapter will conclude with a focused look at the heart of Luke's gospel picture of the forgiving Jesus. Prior to this, a brief glimpse at Luke's Acts of the Apostles will reveal the far-reaching sort of reconciling impact that Luke hoped for as the result of his gospel efforts.

In his letter to the Galatians, Paul stated that the Council of Jerusalem (probably the same meeting that Luke describes in Acts 15) resulted in the following "mission statement."

> Recognizing that I had been entrusted with the gospel for the *uncircumcised*, just as Peter was for the *circumcised* (for he who worked through Peter as his apostle among the Jews had been at work in me for the Gentiles), and recognizing, too, the favor bestowed on me, those who were acknowledged pillars, James,

> Cephas, and John, gave Barnabas and me the handclasp of fellowship, signifying that we should go to the Gentiles as they to the Jews. (Gal 2:7-9).

This "dual mission" to Jew and Gentile is further specified by Luke as a *mission of forgiveness and reconciliation*. First, he shows how Peter attempted to reach the hardened hearts of the people of Israel:

> 'Therefore, let the whole house of Israel know beyond any doubt that God has made both Lord and Messiah this Jesus whom you crucified.' When they heard this, they were deeply shaken. They asked Peter and the other apostles, 'What are we to do, brothers?' Peter answered: 'You must reform and be baptized, each one of you, in the name of Jesus Christ, *that your sins may be forgiven*; then you will receive the gift of the Holy Spirit. It was to you and your children that the promise was made, and to all those still far off whom the Lord our God calls.' (Acts 2:36-39).

At Acts 3:17-21 and 26, Peter "drives a hard bargain" with his fellow Jews: "Therefore, reform your lives! Turn to God, that your sins may be wiped away!" But he packages this challenge with the promise: "Thus may *a season of refreshment* be granted you by the Lord when he sends you Jesus, already designated as your Messiah." Yes, "when God raised up his servant, he sent him to you first to bless you by turning you from your evil ways!"

It might come as somewhat of a surprise to those who are only beginning their study of Luke's Acts to discover that Luke has Peter, not Paul, be the first one to preach the gospel to the Gentiles. (See Acts 10-11, where the Peter-Cornelius encounter is meant to establish Peter's influential role in the Gentile mission.) What is not surprising is the "final touch"

Luke gives to this preaching effort.

> When they heard this (Peter's own account of how the Holy Spirit had come upon the non-Jew, Cornelius, and upon his whole household), the circumcised Jews at Jerusalem stopped objecting, and instead began to glorify God in these words: 'If this be so, then God has granted *life-giving repentance* even to the Gentiles!' (Acts 11:18).

When Luke finally brings Paul into the picture as the *second* "apostle to the Gentiles," he is found preaching to the Jews of the *reconciling effects* of Jesus' life, death, and resurrection:

> We ourselves announce to you the good news that what God promised our fathers he has fulfilled for us, their children, in raising up Jesus, according to what is written in the second psalm, 'You are my son; this day I have begotten you.' As a proof that the one whom he raised from the dead would never again see the decay of death, God declared, 'I will give you the benefits assured to David under the covenant . . . The one whom God has raised up did not undergo corruption. You must realize that it is through him that *the forgiveness of sins* is being proclaimed to you, including the remission of all those charges you could never be acquitted of under the law of Moses. In him, every believer is acquitted. (Acts 13:32-34 and 37-39).

By so presenting both Peter and Paul as missionaries of God's mercy to all peoples, Luke himself becomes "the missionary of reconciliation and forgiveness" in the church! Consequently, the following paraphrase of what he has Peter say in Acts 10:34-36 can well be taken as Luke's own summary understanding of who God is for his people, in Jesus, their Lord. "I now see how true it is that God shows no partiality. Rather, the man or woman of any nation who fears God and acts uprightly is acceptable to him. This is the message he has sent to all his children, the good news of God's mercy and peace proclaimed through Jesus Christ, who is Lord of all!"

We now turn to the heart of Luke's life-giving message of reconciliation, as it appears in his account of Jesus' life and teachings.

The "Merciful Heart" of the Message

Three passages in Luke's gospel reveal the *pattern* of the way he believes sinful people and their merciful God are to relate with each other: the story of the sinner woman who washed Jesus' feet (7:35-52); that of the merciful father and his prodigal sons (15:11-32); and the encounter of Jesus and Zacchaeus, the little tax-collector (19:1-10). (The fact that these passages have already been featured in other sections of this book, e.g., the "sinner woman" in the preceding chapter on *Women And Men In Luke*, only shows how much is contained in each of the small segments of God's word. Indeed, many of Luke's dramatic scenes contain three or four themes within them, enabling the reader to be struck by what she or he "needs to hear" each time the passage is read.) By noticing the pattern in these Lucan scenes of Jesus' attitude toward sinners, and vice-versa, today's "sinful children" of God will learn how to approach him with more confidence and with a special "Lucan spirit."

Notice how all three stories feature sinners who *seem* to take the first step toward making peace with God, with others, and with themselves: the sinner woman enters Simon's house where Jesus is eating and stands weeping behind him (7:38);

the younger son in the parable decides to return to his father to ask for forgiveness, as well as to "take his place as one of his father's hired hands" (15:18-19); Zacchaeus climbs a tree "in order to see Jesus" (19:4). In each dramatic event Luke also describes the murmuring self-righteous ones, who are standing around as Jesus meets the "sinners": "If this man were a prophet, he would know who and what sort of woman this is who touches him — that she is a sinner" (7:38); "For years now I have slaved for you," says the older son to his father, "I have never disobeyed one of your orders, yet you never gave me so much as a kid goat to celebrate with my friends" (15:29); "He (Jesus) has gone to Zacchaeus' house, the house of a sinner, as a guest" (19:7)! But, says Luke, it was to draw sinners to himself and to the Father that Jesus came! Moreover, Luke clearly indicates in each story that the Lord of mercy is always there, always waiting and ready *to take the initiative* with his sinful children, no matter what motivation they might have. For, although Zacchaeus might have climbed the tree "in order to see Jesus" just because he was too small to see him if he had not climbed up there, it was Jesus who looked up and saw him and said: "Zacchaeus, come down! I mean to stay at your house today" (19:5). Likewise, although the younger "sinner son" might have been motivated to return to his father because he was "starving and his father's hired hands had more than enough to eat" (15:17), nonetheless, "While his son was still a long way off, his father caught sight of him and was deeply moved. He ran out to meet him, threw his arms around his neck and kissed him" (15:20). In the third account, Luke has Jesus dialogue with both "sinless Simon" and the "sinner woman" in such a way that it becomes obvious Jesus is the initiator of the healing forgiveness of the woman, and that the whole scene is geared to entice both sinners and sinless ones to be open to God's mercy.

> And Jesus said to Simon: 'Two men owed money to a certain money-lender; one owed a total of five hundred coins, the other fifty. Since neither was able to repay, he wrote off both debts. Which of them was more grateful to him?' Simon answered: 'He, I presume, to whom he remitted the larger sum.' Jesus said to him, 'You are right.' Then, turning to the woman, he said to Simon: 'You see this woman? I came to your home and you provided me with no water for my feet. She has washed my feet with her tears and wiped them with her hair. You did not anoint my head with oil. but she has anointed my feet with perfume. I tell you, *her great love shows that her many sins have been forgiven. The one who is forgiven much, loves much.*' (7:41-47).

(Please note the way the last two sentences are presented here. This seems to be a more accurate rendition of the text, traditionally translated "Her many sins are forgiven because she has loved much. Little is forgiven the one whose love is small." *New American Bible* translation. The italicized version is that of M. Zerwick, who claims that the Greek at this point is ambiguous and can be translated either of the two ways expressed above. However, from the immediate context, namely, the example Jesus gives of the two men whose debts were written off *freely,* in 7:41-42, the meaning of the ambiguous phrase makes more sense and is more in tune with Luke's whole gospel thrust if it is translated as first presented above: "Her great love *shows that* her *many sins have been forgiven.*")

Sinners who know Luke's Jesus can come to their God with trust, knowing that they will be met more than half way. Because of the groundwork Luke has laid in the three gospel accounts just examined, they will be ready to hear what they need to hear: "Your sins are forgiven, now go in peace!" (7:48-50); "Let us eat and celebrate, because this child of mine was dead and has come back to life. He was lost and is found" (15:23f.); "Today salvation has come to this house, for this is what it means to be a child of Abraham. The Son of Man has come to search out and save what was lost!" (19:10).

Christians who attempt to put on a Lucan spirituality of forgiveness will find themselves responding in kind to God's overwhelming mercy. That is, they will experience his pardon with profound *peace, joy,* and *generosity.* They may weep in sorrow for their sins before their God, but they will know the peace that only he can give: "My friend, your sins are forgiven" (see healing of paralytic, 5:17-26). Their confidence may be shaken by others who say "that one is not worthy to be called a Christian," but they will rejoice in remembering how Jesus deemed the sinner woman, the lost son, and Zacchaeus more worthy sharers of his table fellowship than "the sinless Simons" and other righteous ones around them. Thus they will feel free to celebrate with sinners and other forgiven children of God at the banquet he has prepared for them. They will also courageously "stand their ground" as Zacchaeus did and respond generously to Jesus' forgiveness: "I give half of my belongings to the poor" (19:8). They might even become so much like their compassionate Lord that they will learn to reach out to hardened self-righteous ones who murmur against them. Like the father in Jesus' parable, they will "go out and begin to plead with them (the "older sons") to come in and join the celebration of mercy (15:28).

My Child, You Are with Me Always

While sinners of Luke's day were probably able to identify with the forgiven sinners in his gospel, rejoicing in Jesus' forgiving initiative with them, even the "sinless Christians" of then and now are welcome recipients of his good news. To such as these, Luke's Jesus says: "My children, you are with me always and everything I have is yours. Come and celebrate the mercy of God toward all. Come to me for the holiness you seek and you too will come back to life. You can be freed of your anger, resentment, and pride. Let us eat and celebrate, because I am God of *all,* sinners and sinless alike. I want to be in relationship with you . . . if you would just let me! These others, whom you consider unworthy sinners, are all your brothers and sisters. They were dead and have come back to life. 'Be compassionate as your father is compassionate. Do not judge and you will not be judged. Do not condemn and you shall not be condemned. Pardon and you shall be pardoned' (6:36ff.). Come, let us celebrate with our merciful God!"

If the message of Luke's Jesus is taken to heart, Christian discipleship of the twentieth century can truly become a challenging and joyful discipleship of reconciliation. The challenge lies in Christians' *accepting who they are,* as sinners, as well as the reality that sin is a part of human life and a very real part of their relationship with God. The acceptance of this "human and gospel reality" can alleviate the sense of fear and of being "lost souls," which many of God's people feel when they have sinned. The joy comes when Luke's good news of God's mercy brings the sinner into contact with him, *as he is.* As a consequence, like Zacchaeus, the prodigal sons, and the sinner woman of Luke's gospel, God's beloved "sinners" will come to experience the warmth of his fatherly embrace and the power of his enlivening word: "Your sins are forgiven . . . Your faith has been your salvation. Now, go in peace" (7:48 & 50).

Once Christians have experienced God's pardon at the core of their beings, they will much more easily do what Jesus asks: "If your brother or sister does wrong, correct them; if they repent, forgive them. If they sin against you seven times a day, and seven times a day turn back to you saying, "I am sorry," forgive them" (17:3-4). Whether one belongs to the Catholic community of faith, which encourages the experience of reconciliation by a sacramental meeting with God through a priest confessor, or whether one confesses his or her sins before God in some private manner, Luke's good news of God's mercy will help his readers encounter him with peace and confidence. They will be able to join with Peter in saying, with hearts full of joy: "This really is the good news of peace, proclaimed through Jesus Christ, who is Lord of all!" (Acts 10:36).

Part IV

Luke as a Literary Genius

The Spirituality of an Author

Many people try to measure their spirituality or that of others by the way they pray. Actually, a person's spirituality consists as much in how they live and relate to others as in how they pray. In other words, one's relationships with God and with others go hand in hand to make up the whole of one's spiritual life, one's "spirituality." In trying to determine the spirituality of an author, it is important to realize that his or her spirituality comes to be known as much by *how the author's thoughts are expressed* (the structure of the writings) as by *what is actually written down* (the content). In this chapter, a careful look at two "finely tuned" sections of Luke's gospel (the "Infancy Narrative" of cc. 1-2 and the "Journey To Jerusalem Narrative" of 9:51-19:28) will reveal the inner heart of Luke's spirituality. Each narrative will be examined in itself, as an integral part of the entire gospel story's development. Then, when the heartbeat of each section has been listened to , the two narratives will be allowed to stand "side by side," revealing the vibrant source of Luke's relationship with his God and with his people.

1

THE INFANCY NARRATIVE

The First Level: "A Christmas Story"

Luke 1:5-2:52 presents the story of Jesus' birth and childhood in a way that no other evangelist does. With the exception of the accounts of the wise men and the slaughter of the innocents (found only in Mt 2), Luke's story line of the incarnation events has become embedded in the Christian "Christmas consciousness." Only Luke passes on the written memory of the annunciations of the births of John and Jesus. He it is who describes the visit of Mary to Elizabeth, the births of the two baby boys, and the shepherds' visit to the manger in the cave in Bethlehem. The only other "childhood" reminiscences recorded in the gospels, for example, Jesus' presentation in the temple and his being "lost and found" there, come also from Luke's infancy narrative. Likewise, it is Luke's birth account that features Mary, the young maiden whose trust in God moved her from fear to a quiet acceptance and contemplation of the events, "in her heart." Matthew's gospel, on the other hand, highlights the role of Joseph, whose dreams led the holy family to Egypt and back to Galilee. Finally, what would the Christian community do to supplant the unforgettable roles that Zechariah, Anna, and Simeon played in "the beginning of it all?" Yet these characters, along with their prayerful acceptance of Jesus as a child, come to the Christian community only from the pages of Luke's infancy narrative. He was a writer who knew how to choose stories and develop characters that would forever be embedded in the Christian memory.

The Second Level: The Structural Arrangement

However rich and inspiring the first level story line of Luke's infancy narrative may be, there is a second level to his composition that unfolds an even richer depth of meaning to those who recognize it. With *Figure* 2 as a help, Luke's readers are now invited to get into his literary mind and savor his genius.

Each story of the Lucan infancy account has its own power and meaning. For example, the announcement of Jesus' birth (1:26-38) brings out the meaning of trust in God's word through Mary's "Let it be" in the face of such an incredible announcement. At the same time, when this "annunciation" is linked with the second part of a matching, contrasting pair of annunciations (see *Figure* 2), new meaning rushes forth. Now the faith of Mary in her encounter with the angel, Gabriel, is seen in a new light, namely, in contrast with Zechariah's *lack* of trust upon hearing of Elizabeth's preg-

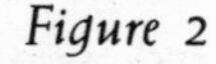

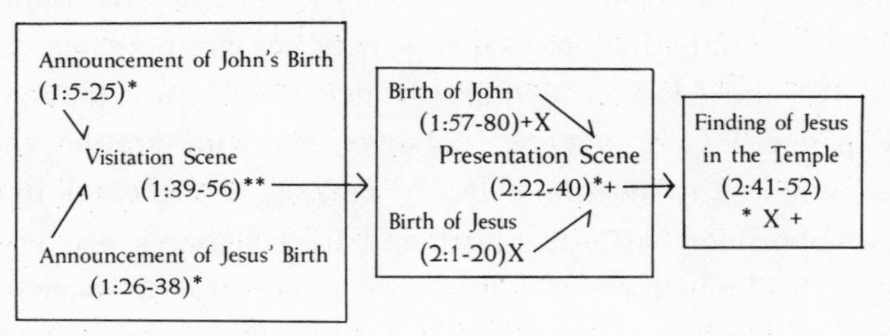

Explanation of symbols:

* = the phrases that express "movement" of the infancy narrative, at 1:23, 38, 39 and 56, 2:39, 51.
+ = the phrase that indicates the gradual growth in age and grace of John and Jesus, at 1:80, 2:40, and 2:52.
X = the phrases that indicate how Mary and others "stored these things up in their hearts," at 1:66, 2:19, and 2:51.

nancy (see 1:18 and 22 in contrast with 1:34 and 38). This striking contrast also highlights the subservient and preparatory role of Zechariah's son, John, to Mary's son, Jesus. This becomes clear when Zechariah proclaims, shortly after his son's birth: "Blessed be the Lord, the God of Israel . . . And you, O child (John), shall be called a prophet of the Most High, for you shall go before the Lord to prepare straight paths for him . . ." (1:68 and 76).

Referring once more to *Figure* 2, careful observers of Luke's intentional structuring of the births, circumcisions, and naming of the two boys almost cries out for comparison (see

1:57-66 and 2:1-21). The two accounts seem to be presented as two parts of one story. Both mothers are favored miraculously: Elizabeth is too far advanced in age to bear a child (1:18) and Mary is a virgin maiden (1:34). Yet, they both experience God's mercy. Moreover, everyone around them experiences an awesome "fear": "Fear descended on all in the neighborhood" at John's birth and at Zechariah's recovery of speech (1:65ff.); the shepherds are quieted by the angel, who proclaims "You have nothing to fear! I come to proclaim good news to you — tidings of joy to be shared by the whole people!" (2:18). All *were* astonished at the report given by the shepherds (2:18). However, at the climax of each birth account lies the contrast! John's birth leaves the people saying: "What will this child be?" and "Was not the hand of the Lord upon him?" (1:66). Jesus' birth results in Mary's "treasuring all these things in her heart" and the shepherds' "glorifying and praising God for all they had seen and heard" (2:19-20). Salvation had come to the world in the birth of the one named *Jesus* (2:21)! John's role is already firmly established at his birth! And Luke's readers know the answer to the question the crowd asked about John (in 1:66). He will be the "preparer of the way" for Jesus, both in his adult years as in his birth!

The paired announcement and birth stories, often referred to as "doublets," are each followed by special scenes that further the deeper meaning of Luke's infancy narrative, namely, the scenes of the visitation and the presentation of Jesus in the temple (1:39-56 and 2:22-40). By itself, Mary's visit to Elizabeth brings out her dignity as the future mother of God: "Blest are you among women and blest is the fruit of your womb" (1:42). The account of Jesus' presentation in the temple, in itself, emphasized the dignity and role of Jesus as "the light to the Gentiles and the glory of Israel" (2:32). There is enough richness of beauty and significance in each story as it stands alone. When, however, they are witnessed "as a pair" in Luke's structure, they become even more evocative moments. They become proclamations to the whole world that what is happening here is the dawning of salvation: first, a beloved *relative,* Elizabeth, hears the news; then, Simeon and Anna, faithful *descendants of Israel,* hear it; finally, all of Israel and the Gentile world share in Simeon's vision . . . "God's saving deed is displayed (in Jesus) for *all the peoples* to see" (2:30f.).

One more glance at *Figure* 2 shows that there is one story that "does not fit" into the doublet-plus proclamation scheme of Luke's structure. It is the last event of the infancy narrative, the finding of Jesus in the temple (2:41-52). It stands alone, with no matching story. Consequently, its status as the only "unmatched story" within Luke's infancy account draws special attention to itself. Its climactic "last" position also gives the reader a hint of its importance. What is the unique conclusion to this tightly knit introduction to Luke's gospel? Will it possibly summarize all that has come before it? Might it also be "the keynote" for all that will follow? Let the readers of Luke discover that for themselves by looking closely at these ten verses.

The scene is set in verses 41-47. Joseph and Mary had brought Jesus on the customary family trip to Jerusalem to celebrate the Passover. Jesus was twelve years old. In the caravan of families on the way home, his parents presumed that he was with some of their friends or relatives. In fact, he had stayed in Jerusalem. Two days later, after searching for him, they find him amazing the teachers in the temple with his questions and responses. The ensuing dialogue and its consequences are what Luke's infancy narrative has been leading up to. The very normal mother expresses her upset feelings with her son: "Son, why have you done this to us? You see that your father and I have been searching for you in sorrow" (2:48). Instead of saying he is sorry, Jesus responds: "Why did you search for me? Did you not know that I had to be in my Father's house?" (2:49). On the surface level, Jesus' words are an affront to his parents' feelings. On another level, he could be understood to have meant: "You should have known I would be in *this place,* and therefore you need not have searched elsewhere and worried so." However, in the context of the whole Lucan gospel, that is, in "the whole picture," it is obviously Luke's intention to lead his readers to a third level of meaning. That third level of meaning has to do with Jesus' relationship to his Father, to his mother, and the will of God for all of his children. *This* is the "keynote" of the whole gospel message, as Luke's readers have already seen in Part Two of this book: to "be in my Father's house," to "be about my Father's business." This is what Jesus is about. This is who Jesus is! The final box in *Figure 2,* to which all the arrows finally point, is the "relational box." Jesus is the son of Mary and Joseph: "Your father and I have been searching for you in sorrow." But he is more. He is also the son of God, and God is also a father! His heavenly Father is the one whom Jesus, as well as Jesus' earthly mother and step-father, are to search out and obey. "But they did not grasp what he said to them" (2:50).

The scene of mother-finding-son-in-Father's-house ends with the verses: "He went down with them then, and came to Nazareth, and was obedient to them. His mother meanwhile kept all these things in memory. Jesus, for his part, progressed steadily in wisdom and age and grace before God and everyone else" (2:51f.). At the end of the gospel, in two other climactic passages, Luke's Jesus will once again center his *whole* life on his Father and his Father's will for him. This happens in the garden, when Jesus prays "*Father,* if it is your will, take this cup from me; yet not my will, but yours be done" (22:42). And finally, when it is clear that he has "been about his Father's business," Jesus cries out from the cross: "*Father,* into your hands I commend my spirit" (23:46). (One can detect the intention of Luke to emphasize the "Father connection" of this "cross statement" with the "finding in the temple story," because Luke adapts the cry of the Psalmist (Ps 31:6) from "Into your hands I commend my spirit; you will redeem me, O Lord, O faithful God" to "*Father,* into your hands . . .") What began in the Jerusalem temple as a single-minded, relational commitment to God, as Father, ends on the cross in Jerusalem as fruit of Jesus' growing in wisdom, age, and grace, as his Father's son! And although Mary "did not grasp what he said to them" in the Jerusalem temple, through her contemplation of "all these things," she would come to be among those few trusting ones who would gather in Jerusalem, devoting themselves to constant prayer, after Jesus' resurrection (Acts 1:14). The final scene of Luke's infancy narrative not only summarizes what has led up to it, it also functions as a dramatic introduction to *the meaning of discipleship and relationship with God* as it unravels in the whole gospel and Acts of Luke. As Jesus is dedicated to being an obedient son of his Father, so will his mother be. So must be any Lucan son or daughter on pilgrimage to the heavenly "house" of their Father!

Yet a Third Level: The Refrains

Being in touch with the "paired story" structural arrangement of Luke's first two chapters leads his readers to "total dedication to their Father's will." The three refrains found in these chapters (see *+X symbols in *Figure* 2) also have a deeper meaning than that which meets the eye. As the reader studies how and where these three phrases occur, one can sense something of a cumulative effect. First comes the "*movement language*" (*) as each of the first three sections of the infancy account has people "going home" (Zechariah, in 1:23), "leaving" (angel, in 1:38), "setting out" and "returning home" (Mary, in 1:39 and 56). A fifth instance of this is found at the end of the presentation scene, when Mary and Joseph "returned to Galilee and their own town of Nazareth" (2:39). The final occurance of this motion language is in 2:51, in the climactic scene in the temple, when Jesus "went down with them, and came to Nazareth, and was obedient to them." Then comes the "*gradual growth terminology*" (+). This appears in the second stage of the infancy narrative, as both John and Jesus "grew up and matured in spirit . . . in size and strength, filled with wisdom, and the grace of God" (1:80 and 2:40). The third and final mention of the same theme comes in the very last line of the entire infancy account, which is also the conclusion of the scene of the finding of Jesus in the temple: "Jesus, for his part, progressed steadily in wisdom and age and grace before God and everyone else" (2:52). The third refrain that stands out in Luke's first two chapters is *"she/they stored all these things in her/their heart(s)"* (X). One notes that this is the concluding phrase of the matching birth accounts (in 1:66 and 2:19), and, as might well be expected, it also makes its final appearance at 2:51b, when Mary is characterized as "keeping all these things in memory."

As the reader of Luke's infancy story comes across each of these refrains, the constant movement of the drama and the prayerful growth in God's Spirit is obvious. However, when all of the refrains are followed out in their place in Luke's structural arrangement, they take on a progressively deeper meaning. They are not just historical notes about what happened. They are not just "transitional phrases" that enable the author to move from one story to the next smoothly. They are heavily laden symbols-in-words, signals for the alert person of faith to enter into the journey of growth and prayer with Jesus, Mary, and all the characters that surrounded the incarnation event. It is especially when one concentrates on the summary point, in 2:51-52, where all three refrains come together, that Luke's purpose is clearly unveiled. First, "to be in his Father's house" is the primary task of Jesus and all his followers. But "doing the Father's will" is an activity that goes on in the real life situations in which Christians find themselves: "Jesus went down with them, and came to Nazareth, and was obedient to them" (2:51a). Secondly, the will of God is not always immediately clear and discernible, even to the holiest among God's people. Contemplating and remembering God's ways of dealing with his people often reveals his deeper purpose, only in time and in further unfolding events. So even though she did not grasp what Jesus said to her, "Mary kept all these things in memory" (2:51b). Finally, if even Jesus had to "progress steadily in wisdom, age, and grace" (2:52), how much more are his followers to be encouraged to take their development as Christian disciples seriously! With Mary and Jesus, Luke's readers might well conclude this examination of Luke 1-2 by reflecting on a passage from Isaiah 43, which both expresses who their Father is and what he has in store for them, his children.

> Because you are precious in my eyes and glorious, and because I love you, I give men in return for you and peoples in exchange for your life. Fear not, for I am with you . . . Everyone who is named as mine, whom I created for my glory, whom I formed and made, I will bring back: my sons from afar and my daughters from the ends of the earth . . . See, I am doing something new! Now it springs forth, do you not perceive it? In the desert I make a way, in the wasteland, rivers. (Is 43:4-6, 19).

Indeed, as the infancy narrative comes to an end, Luke's audience is swept along into the desert to meet the "full grown" John (3:1-6). Through his message of "baptism of repentance which leads to the forgiveness of sins" (3:3), they are also ready to meet the mature Jesus, the "one on whom the Father's favor rests" (3:22). After joining Jesus in his "desert experience" (4:1-13), twentieth century Christians will be better prepared to join him on the rest of his journey, namely, on his "journey to Jerusalem."

2

THE JOURNEY TO JERUSALEM NARRATIVE

Experts on Luke's writings have, for some time, referred to chapters 9 through 19 of his gospel as "Luke's Journey Narrative." It is called *Luke's* narrative because much of the material in these chapters is not preserved by the other gospel writers. For example, Jesus' well-known parables of The Good Samaritan and The Prodigal Son appear in this section (10:25-37 and 15:11-32). Likewise, some of the fascinating characters that appear on Jesus' way, like Martha and Mary (10:38-42), the badly stooped woman in the synagogue (13:10-17), and the tax collector, Zacchaeus (19:1-10), are remembered only by Luke. This section is called Luke's *journey* narrative because careful study has revealed that, at 9:51, Luke has departed from the "order of events" found in one of his written sources (Mark's gospel) in order to plot a deliberate journey "up to Jerusalem." (See the asterisks in *Figure 3,* which indicate the beginning, at 9:51, the high point, at 13:33, and the ending, at

19:28, of this Lucan "journey to Jerusalem.") It is after Jesus "went ahead with his ascent to Jerusalem," that Luke takes up his written source (Mark's gospel) once more. He then follows, more or less, the sequence of events which is similar to that of Mark and Matthew, namely, the order of events leading up to the passion and death of Jesus.

The Lucan composition of 9:51-19:28 is a masterpiece of literary art. Even without the help of *Figure* 3, which depicts the structural balance of passages and themes, the "journey to Jerusalem" chapters read beautifully. There is a progressive "flow" to the drama. There is also a constant "reflection back" to earlier parts of Luke's gospel, which enables the reader to experience a sense of continuity with all that has come before. For example, the "journey passages" concerning prayer and trust, in 11:1-13 and 12:13-34, remind the reader of Mary's prayer of profound faith in the infancy narrative. However, what is fascinating to note is the pattern of parallel images and passages that "go up" and "come down" (see *Figure* 3). Unlike the structure of the infancy narrative, which progressed "from left to right" (recall *Figure* 2), in linear fashion, this journey section is structured more like a mountain, with the themes of the upward climb being repeated as one descends, only *in reverse order!* Consequently, when one reads "down," from F' through A', after having read "up," from A through F, the experience is much like watching an instant replay on television, only backwards! It is as if Luke wants his readers to cover exactly the same ground a second time, except from a different angle, from a slightly different perspective or point of view. And what holds it all together is the thread of "I must proceed on course . . . to Jerusalem," the *top* of the "mountain structure" (13:33) and the *purpose* of the entire composition (9:51 and 19:28)!

Figure 3

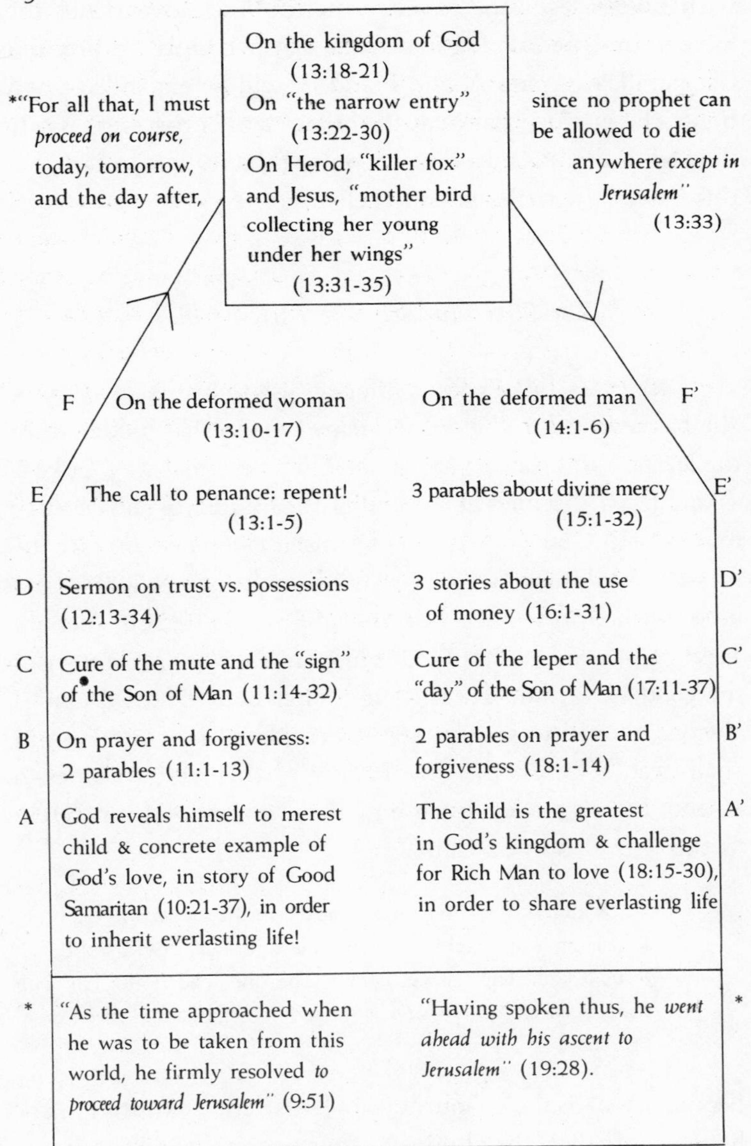
On the kingdom of God (13:18-21)
On "the narrow entry" (13:22-30)
On Herod, "killer fox" and Jesus, "mother bird collecting her young under her wings" (13:31-35)
*"For all that, I must *proceed on course,* today, tomorrow, and the day after,
since no prophet can be allowed to die anywhere *except in Jerusalem*" (13:33)
F On the deformed woman (13:10-17)
On the deformed man (14:1-6) F'
E The call to penance: repent! (13:1-5)
3 parables about divine mercy (15:1-32) E'
D Sermon on trust vs. possessions (12:13-34)
3 stories about the use of money (16:1-31) D'
C Cure of the mute and the "sign" of the Son of Man (11:14-32)
Cure of the leper and the "day" of the Son of Man (17:11-37) C'
B On prayer and forgiveness: 2 parables (11:1-13)
2 parables on prayer and forgiveness (18:1-14) B'
A God reveals himself to merest child & concrete example of God's love, in story of Good Samaritan (10:21-37), in order to inherit everlasting life!
The child is the greatest in God's kingdom & challenge for Rich Man to love (18:15-30), in order to share everlasting life A'
* "As the time approached when he was to be taken from this world, he firmly resolved *to proceed toward Jerusalem*" (9:51)
"Having spoken thus, he *went ahead with his ascent to Jerusalem*" (19:28). *

Luke's readers are now invited to "climb the mountain" with Luke's Jesus and to allow themselves to experience the force of this special section of Luke's gospel. Only the first and last parallels, A and A' and F and F', will be expanded upon here. The cursory glance at the other parallel passages (B & B' through E & E') is meant to encourage the readers to carry on this "ascent with Jesus" on their own.

The First Parallel: The Merest Child

In 10:21-24 Luke's Jesus offers praise to his *Father* because "he has revealed to the *merest children* what he has hidden from the learned and the clever" (v. 21). In a very real way, Luke is asking Jesus' disciples at the end of the first Christian century to rejoice in God's revelation of himself *to them* — *they* are the blessed "children," who see and hear "what prophets and kings wished to see and hear, but did not" (10:24)! Then, in 10:25-37, they see what God is like, in Jesus' example story of the good Samaritan. He is their compassionate healer, who is always "moved to pity" when his children are wounded and "half-dead" (vv. 30 and 33). Finally, as this section comes to an end, Luke's readers learn how they can respond concretely to this "revelation of God":

> 'Which of the three who came down the road from Jericho to Jerusalem was neighbor to the one who fell in with robbers?' Jesus asked. The answer came, 'The one who *treated him with compassion.' Jesus then said to the scribe, 'Then go and do likewise.'* (10:36f.).

Section A of Luke's "journey to Jerusalem" narrative highlights the Father, the child, and the concrete manifestation of the Father's love for his people in Jesus, the perfect "good Samaritan." Paralleling section A is section A', which occurs near the end of the journey narrative, at 18:15-30. A' begins much like A.

> They even brought *babies* to be touched by him. When the disciples saw this, they scolded him roundly. But Jesus called for the children, saying 'Let the little children come to me. Do not shut them off. The reign of God belongs to such as these. Trust me when I tell you that whoever does not accept the kingdom of God *as a child* will not enter it.' (18:15-17).

Section A' continues by showing God's children how to act out this "childlike trust," as Luke presents the encounter between Jesus and the rich ruler.

> You have kept all the commandments *since you were a boy* — there is one thing further you must do. Sell all that you have and give to the poor. You will have treasure in heaven. Then, come and follow me. (18:21-22).

Luke's section A' thus repeats the same message as section A. Even though it is "easier for a camel to go through a needle's eye than for a rich person to enter the kingdom of heaven" (18:25), things that are seemingly impossible are possible for God (18:27) and for those who trust in him *like his children*, letting go of worldly possessions and sharing their love with those in need! This is the way to inherit and to share in everlasting life (10:27; 18:20)!!

Such a "double emphasis" on trust and concrete love of neighbor, as seen in A and A', suggests the importance Luke wants to give to these Christian attributes. However basic they are, Luke goes on to "flesh out" the meaning of Christian trust and love in the other parallels of his journey narrative.

Persistent prayer for God's mercy (B') follows upon the corresponding mercy that Christians show one another ("Father, forgive us our sins for we too forgive all who do us wrong," in B, at 11:4). The Son of Man, Jesus, has preceded his followers on the journey, as their healer (see C and C' cures of the mute and the leper), but Christians have to reform their lives (11:32, in C) and "lose them" for the sake of the kingdom (17:33, in C'), if they wish to be judged favorably when the Son of Man comes at the end of time. Dependence on God's providence, rather than on riches (12:22-31, in D), will make the journey of Christians a generous *and* a profitable one, since they will "eat bread in the kingdom of God" (14:15, in D'). Repentance for sin (13:1-5, in E) and the conversion of one sinner's heart (15:7 & 10, in E') will bring more joy in heaven "than ninety-nine righteous people who have no need to repent!"

The Last Parallel: The Deformed Woman and Man

The final parallel on *Figure* 3 features a woman (F, 13:10-17) and a man (F', 14:1-6). Each suffers from a severe physical disease. Each encounters Jesus on the Sabbath. With both of them, Jesus takes the healing initiative. "When Jesus saw the badly stooped woman, who for eighteen years had been possessed by a spirit which drained her strength, he called her to him and said 'Woman, you are free of your iniquity' " (13:11f.). "Directly in front of him was a man who suffered from dropsy. He asked the lawyers and the Pharisees 'Is it lawful to cure on the Sabbath or not?' At this they kept silent. He took the man, healed him, and sent him on his way"

(14:2ff.). By these two "paired stories" of Jesus' outreach in healing love, Luke is stressing his conviction that both women and men, weary of what keeps them from standing erect before God or others, can take hope and courage from Jesus. He knows their suffering and depression. He considers them more important than "keeping the Sabbath." He will bring them to his kingdom, whole and happy, if they stay with him "to the top of the mountain."

The Climax: The Kingdom of God

There is "a method in Luke's madness," that is, in his arrangement of his gospel in this A and A', B and B', etc., way. All of the parallel passages, which emphasize important values of Jesus, hinge on the balance, on the centerpiece, on the climax in 13:18-35. Here, in vivid imagery, Luke features the kingdom of God, which "resembles a mustard seed, the smallest of all the plants, yet grows to be so large that it is a place for the birds of the air to nest in" (13:19). This kingdom also has a dynamic growth about it, like the bit of yeast that makes flour rise into a whole mass of dough (13:21). The kingdom is not easily attainable: "Try to come in through the narrow door" (13:24). It is *not* for those presumptuous ones who claim they know the Lord (13:25-28). It *is* for those "surprised guests" at the feast, the ones looked on as "outsiders" (13:29). Indeed, those who are considered the least or last, shall be the first, "and the first shall be last" (13:30)! Luke, of course, was warning Jesus' Jewish country men and women that "being a Jew or a Christian does not automatically bring one into the kingdom. Rather, his kingdom is for those who go with and *grow with* Jesus, no matter what their racial background or religious affiliation might be." Today, Luke's message about the kingdom is as challenging to Christians as it was in the first century. This is especially true for those who presume to "have it made": "After all, I am a Christian. I have been baptized and profess that Jesus is Lord. I go to church regularly. What more is needed?"

"What more is needed" is total allegiance to the Lord of the kingdom, whom Luke describes at this climactic juncture in the most moving terms. In contrast to "Herod, that fox," who is out to kill him, Jesus cries out: "Jerusalem, Jerusalem . . . How often I have wanted to gather *your children* together *as a mother bird* collects her young under her wings, and you refused me!" (13:34). No single Christian virtue required for the Christian journey, not even the whole lot of them described in Luke's gospel and Acts, is sufficient! Only an intimate, dedicated, deeply personal relationship with Jesus makes the journey's end possible! Yes, at the height of his gospel message stands Luke's Jesus, the one who longs to hold his disciples of all times very close to himself. If the kingdom of God is like the mustard bush, whose branches provide a place for the birds of the air to rest in, how appropriate that Jesus be imaged by Luke as the mother bird, longing to gather her young under her wings. By accepting Jesus with the utter dependence of the baby bird, mature Christians discover the secret of the kingdom of God. With Jesus, all is possible! This is the climax of Luke's "journey to Jerusalem" narrative, both in content and in structure. It is the heartbeat of Lucan spirituality.

3

THE TWO MASTERPIECES: SIDE BY SIDE

To conclude this examination of Luke's literary genius, the two narratives of the infancy and journey of Jesus are placed side by side. (See *Figure 4* below.) As Luke's readers can see, the two climaxes surprisingly converge on one message: being a Lucan Christian means *being in relationship with God as Father,* in the same way that the son and the mother were! This is the secret to the entry to the kingdom!

According to Luke, both Mary, the mother, and Jesus the son, learned and lived the secret to God's kingdom. That secret, their relationship with God as Father, brought them both, weeping, to the temple in Jerusalem. The distressed mother searched there for her lost son (2:48). Then came the son lamenting like "a mother bird over her young," over the city and the people, who had refused him (13:34b). That secret

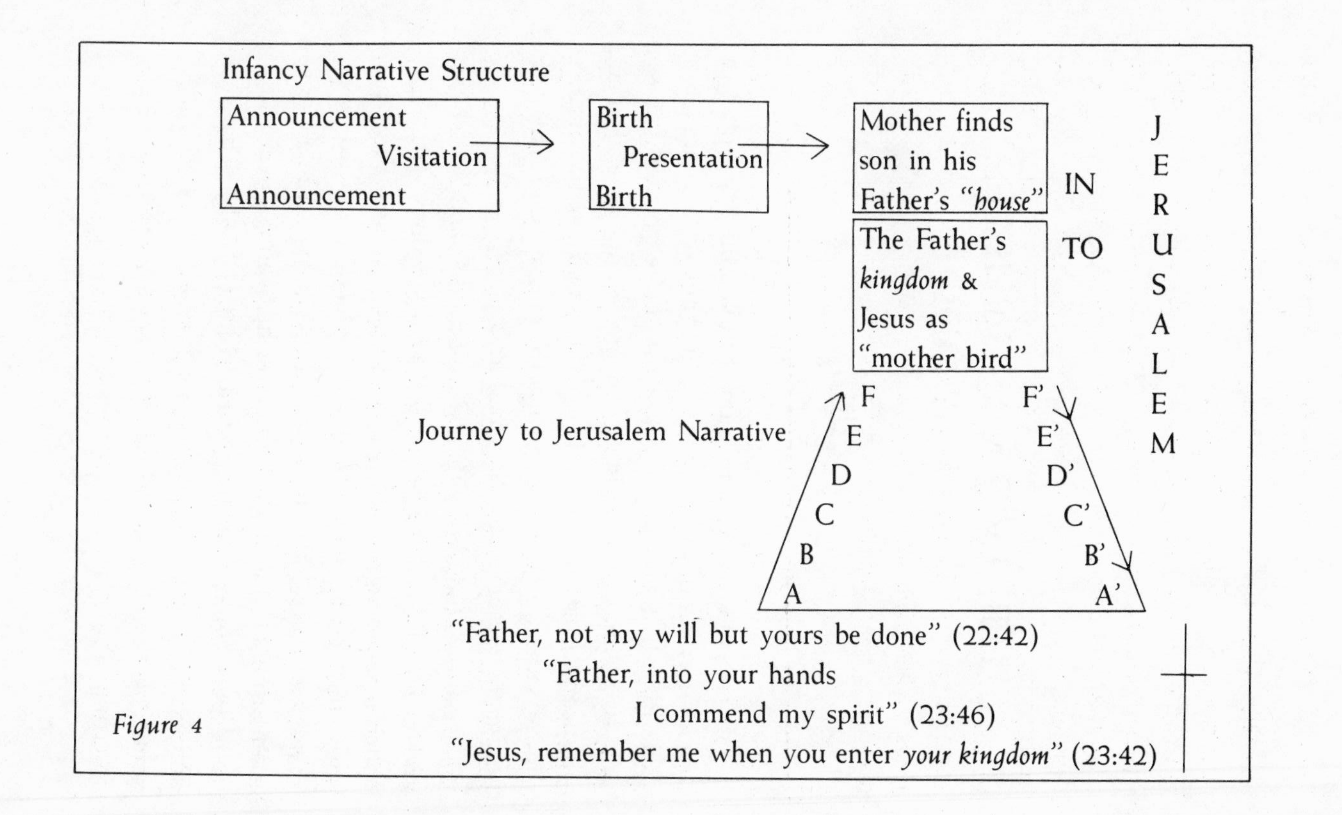
Infancy Narrative Structure
Announcement
Visitation
Announcement
Birth
Presentation
Birth
Mother finds
son in his
Father's "*house*"
The Father's
kingdom &
Jesus as
"mother bird"
IN
TO
JERUSALEM
Journey to Jerusalem Narrative
F
E
D
C
B
A
F'
E'
D'
C'
B'
A'
"Father, not my will but yours be done" (22:42)
"Father, into your hands
I commend my spirit" (23:46)
"Jesus, remember me when you enter *your kingdom*" (23:42)
Figure 4

was also unveiled in Jerusalem. First, in Jesus' mysterious response to his mother "Why did you search for me? Did you not know that I had to be in my Father's house?" (2:49). Then, in his reproach of the city "O Jerusalem, Jerusalem, you slay the prophets and stone those who are sent to you" (13:34a). And finally, in the clear, loud cry from the cross "Father, into your hands I commend my spirit" (23:46). Both mother and son had consecrated themselves to a life-long commitment to their Lord and Father (Mary in 1:38, and Jesus in 2:49 and 22:42). Whatever they did or said, it was always as his confident children, even unto death.

As maturing Christian men and women try to model their lives on Jesus and Mary today, they can learn much from Luke's infancy and journey narratives. They can discover anew the very personal and relational nature of their Christian faith. It was this relational faith and love that sustained Jesus and Mary on their journeys. And they are now one with the Father in fullness, awaiting their brothers and sisters, who continue on the journey. It is this same child-Father relationship that gives meaning to *all* of one's life. Luke's profound insight into the Christian life says clearly: "it is not so much *what* you do as *who* you are and *how you relate* to your Father and to his other children." And although he provides many concrete suggestions for being creative and loving in relationship, the heart and soul of Luke's spirituality is that which makes us Christian, namely, "in Jesus Christ, God has become a Father to us all!"

Besides a prayerful rereading of Luke's chapters, just examined in these pages of Part Four, his readers might also profit by spending some quality time with two of Luke's forerunners, the prophets Isaiah and Hosea. Their prophetic words to the people of Sion in exile can only enliven one's experience of God as an ever loving Father and "Mother." Some excerpts from Isaiah 49 and Hosea 11 will help those who feel the need to be drawn into the loving embrace of their God.

> Can a mother forget her infant, be without tenderness for the child of her womb? Even should she forget, I will never forget you. See, upon the palms of my hands I have written your name; your walls are ever before me. Your rebuilders make haste, as those who tore you down and laid you waste go forth from you. Look about you and see, they are all gathering and coming to you (Jerusalem). As I live, says the Lord, you shall be arrayed with them all as with adornments, like a bride you shall fasten them on you. (Is 49:15-18)

> See, I will lift up my hand to the nations, and raise my signal to the peoples; they shall bring your sons in their arms, and your daughters shall be carried on their shoulders. Kings shall be your foster fathers, their princesses your nurses; bowing to the ground, they shall worship you and lick the dust at your feet. Then you shall know that I am the Lord, and those who hope in me shall never be disappointed. (Is 49:22f.).

> When Israel was a child I loved him, out of Egypt I called my son . . . It was I who taught Ephraim to walk, who took them in my arms; I drew them with human cords, with bands of love; I fostered them like one who raises an infant to his cheeks . . . My heart is overwhelmed; my pity is stirred . . . Out of Egypt they shall come trembling, like sparrows, from the land of Assyria, like doves; and I will resettle them in their homes, says the Lord. (Hosea 11:1-4, 8c ,11.).

Part V

More Lucan Themes for the Journey

1

"YOUR KINGDOM COME"

Every day, in every country around the world, Christians pray the Our Father, "as Jesus has taught us." They pray that the Father's name "be hallowed," that is, reverenced. They pray for their "daily bread," and that God forgive them their sins as they forgive others. The second petition of Luke's version of the Our Father reads simply: "Your kingdom come!" (11:2). However brief that petition may be, it is laden with meaning. It expresses the Christian hope that God's kingdom of peace, love, and forgiveness will come soon. It embodies humanity's longing for all that is good and satisfying for the family of God. It also begs for response to the questions: "How and when will this kingdom come?" And depending on how each Christian answers these questions, his or her spiritual outlook on life will vary dramatically. Twentieth century Christians can look to Luke to help them fix their eyes on God's kingdom in a way that will be healing and salvific in their contemporary world.

The Kingdom Is Coming Tomorrow: Mark, Matthew, and Paul

In the first Christian century there existed a variety of understandings of how and when the kingdom of God would come. One view is emphasized by the gospels of Mark and Matthew, as well as by Paul, in his letters to the Thessalonians and the Corinthians. This view stressed the early return of Jesus in his glory, and with it, the establishment of God's kingdom in power.

> If anyone in this faithless and corrupt age is ashamed of me and of my doctrine, the Son of Man will be ashamed of him when he comes with the holy angels in his Father's glory. I assure you, among those standing here there are some who will not face death *until they see the kingdom of God established in power.* (Mark 8:38-9:1; Mt 16:27f.; see also Lk 9:27).

This stark warning and promise came at a high point of Jesus' earthly ministry, at Caesarea Philippi, just after his first prediction of his coming death and resurrection. The impact of this understanding of Jesus' immanent return in glory was powerful indeed. For example, Matthew, who shares this view, urged his community of faith to be very watchful for Jesus' return.

> Keep a watchful eye and be prepared. The Son of Man is coming at the time you least expect. Who is the faithful, far-sighted servant whom the master has put in charge of his household to dispense food at need? Happy the servant whom his master discovers at work on his return. I assure you, he will put him in charge of all his property. (Mt 24:44-48).

Matthew's Jesus was responding to the question: "What will be the sign of your coming and the end of the world?" (24:3). He had first replied:

> Be on guard. Let no one mislead you. False messiahs will come. Wars and famine and earthquakes will happen in many places. Such things are bound to happen, but that is not yet the end. These are early stages of the birth pangs. They will hand you over to torture you and to kill you. Indeed, you will be hated by all the nations on my account . . . Because of the increase of evil, the love of most will grow cold. The one who holds out to the end, however, is the one who will see salvation. This good news of the kingdom will be proclaimed throughout the world as a witness to all the nations. Only after that will the end come. (Mt 24:3-14).

With these two passages, two new facets are seen in this understanding of Jesus' imminent *parousia* (the Greek word for Jesus' second coming). First, it seems that Jesus' coming will not only usher in his Father's kingdom, but also the end of the world. Secondly, although the exact time is unknown, this end, this coming, this kingdom will not come until the gospel has been preached to all the nations. One might believe, at first hearing all this, that Matthew is saying that the kingdom will actually be long in coming, since even today, some twenty centuries later, "all the nations" have not yet heard the good news. However, when one goes on to read the next section of chapter 24, it becomes clear that it was Matthew's first century hope that his contemporaries would be the ones to bring that word to all. Consequently, they would also be the ones to see God's kingdom established in power, in their time.

> Immediately after the stress of that period (as described in vv. 15-28), the sun will be darkened, the moon will not shed her light, the stars will fall from the sky, and the hosts of heaven will be shaken loose. Then the sign of the Son of Man will appear in the sky, and all the clans of the earth will strike their breasts as they see the Son of Man coming on the clouds of heaven with power and great glory. He will dispatch his angels with a mighty trumpet blast, and they will assemble his chosen from the four winds, from one end of the heavens to the other. From the fig tree learn a lesson. When its branch grows tender and sprouts leaves, you realize that the summer is near. Likewise, when you see all these things happening, you will know that he is near, standing at your door. I assure you, the present generation will not pass away until all this take place. (Mt 24:29-34; Mk 13:30; see also Lk 21:32ff.).

The tone of this Matthean view of Jesus' "tomorrow return" in glory urges those who share his expectation to an all embracing, radical, "now response." Paul expresses it this way: "May the Lord increase you and make you overflow with love for one another and for all, even as our love does for you. May he strengthen your hearts and make them blameless and holy before our God and Father at the coming of our Lord Jesus with all his holy ones!" (1 Thes 3:12f). Believing that Jesus' return was "just around the corner" explains what lies behind Paul's strange-sounding demands of 1 Corinthians 7:

> I tell you, brothers and sisters, the time is short. From now on those with wives should live as though they had none; those who weep should live as though they were not weeping; those who rejoice as though they were not rejoicing; buyers should conduct themselves as though they owned nothing, and those who make use of the world as though they were not using it, for the world as we know it is passing away. (vv. 29-31).

Those Christians who espouse this view of Jesus' immanent return today, along with the belief that the end of the world and establishment of God's kingdom come along with it, have something to offer. In this time of nuclear threat, it is as if God's kingdom must be established soon, or else there may not be any earth on which to establish it! At the same time, in all its urgency, this "hurry up" brand of spirituality can become distorted if it becomes a fear-inspiring, judgmental, "prediction of the last days" brand of Christianity. This caution comes even from the Matthean, Marcan, and Pauline writings that encouraged urgency, *while at the same time* pleading for calm trust. "As to the exact day or hour, no one knows it, neither the angels in heaven, nor even the Son, but only the Father" (Mk 13:32 & Mt 24:36). It is as if this tradition of the first Christian century would sum up its belief in this way: "Watch for the kingdom! Be on guard for Jesus' return! Be ready for the end! But do all this with confidence in God, who will bring it about in his own time. And cooperate with him, by gracious love for one another and for all!"

The Kingdom Is "Now and Not Yet": Luke and John and Paul

At more or less the same time that Mark and Matthew were proclaiming their message, Luke was handing on another early Christian tradition about the coming of the kingdom. While he also urged his community to be watchful for the appearance of God's kingdom (9:27; 21:32ff.), he develops something new in his gospel and Acts. It involves the Spirit. It responds to the fact that many "first generation Christians" had died without seeing the power of the kingdom established on earth. It is phrased most strikingly in this way:

> You cannot tell by careful watching when the reign of God will come. Neither is it a matter of reporting that it is 'here' or 'there.' The reign of God is already in your midst! (Lk 17:20f.).

Here, in Jesus' punch line, "the reign of God is already here," Luke has not put aside all expectations regarding the future coming of God's kingdom. Indeed, Luke wanted his community to do all in its power to bring about the fullness of that kingdom. But, he says, it is *now, today,* that the kingdom is here! It is *already within* God's people by the power of the Holy Spirit. And by the Spirit of the risen Lord, God is moving his people towards the fullness!

What a dramatic shift in perspective: from "the kingdom is coming tomorrow" to "the kingdom is already within"! Luke therefore brings his readers into a healthy "already *but not yet fully* here" tension concerning God's kingdom on earth. He was not the first to do so. Paul's later letters had emphasized the presence of Christ and the Spirit within the Christian person and church. Nor was Luke the last inspired writer to say "now and not yet" in regard to the kingdom. John's gospel, written some ten to twenty years later than Luke, would also emphasize the "kingdom already present" view. Nonetheless, it is Luke who expresses it best, or at least, most explicitly. For example, Luke is far more deliberate in his use of the words "today" and "now." "*Today* salvation has come to this house," Luke's Jesus says to the tax collector (19:10, in *Journey B*). But it had already come in *Journey A,* the story of Israel! "*Today* in the town of David a savior has been born to you" (2:11). Jesus' first sermon ended on such a note: "*Today* this scripture passage has been fulfilled in your midst" (4:21). His next-to-last word from the cross was the same: "*Today* you will be with me in paradise" (23:43). In *Journey* C Paul wished "before God, that all who had heard him *today* would come to be as he was," namely, a new person in Christ (Acts 26:29). Paul was also a "now person" in Christ. In the Acts, he cries out: "*Now* (is the time that) God is telling everyone, everywhere, to reform their lives!" (17:30). It almost seems that Luke wants to draw the future and the past into the present. For example, he has Stephen address certain Jews, many years after Jesus' death: "*Now* you have become the Just One's betrayers, his murderers" (Acts 7:52). Christian time is "now." The time of God's kingdom is "now." For Jesus lives! He has been raised from the dead! He is alive among the members of his church in the Spirit! And he is alive, not only with Simeon, who prayed "*Now,* Master, you can let your servant go in peace" (2:29), but with all his servants. He has life, not only in the womb of Mary, but also in the womb of the church that bears his name: "*From this day forward,* all generations shall call me blessed!" (1:48). For Luke, the "today" and the "now" of God's presence with his people in Jesus is the *key part of the process* that extended through Jesus' life to his death and resurrection and into the life of the church-in-time. Luke's brand of spirituality does not, therefore, inspire fear about tomorrow. It inspires the Spirit-filled church to come to terms, eagerly, with its continuing existence and responsibility in the world. God's kingdom truly is like yeast "that makes the whole mass of dough rise" and like the tiny mustard seed "that grows and becomes the resting place for the birds of the air" (13:18-21).

Two final texts bring out the force of Luke's "now spirituality." The shift from an emphasis on the future coming of Christ and his kingdom to living the Christian life now "as children of the kingdom" literally jumps off the page in chapter 9 of his gospel. There, in contrast to Matthew and Mark who record that Jesus said: "If anyone wishes to follow me, they must take up their cross and follow in my steps" (Mk 8:34 & Mt 16:24), Luke has Jesus say: "Let Christians take up their cross *daily* and follow me!" (9:23)! The Lucan addition of the one word, daily, focuses the whole Christian life project. It is daily that followers of Jesus establish his kingdom on earth. It is in day-to-day deaths to themselves that they manifest Jesus' life and power. No longer is God's kingdom to be thought of solely as the reward that comes only at the end, after one's death. With each act of loving service, in imitation of Jesus, Christians make the kingdom present! One further Lucan adaptation of a passage he shares with Matthew and Mark pleads his cause for a day-to-day experience of God's kingdom. All three evangelists encourage their congregations to endure all sorts of hardships in their Christian mission, even though they will be hated by everyone. Matthew and Mark end this section by saying: "For the one who *holds out until the end* is the one who will come through safely" (Mk 13:13 & Mt 10:22). Luke concludes: "*By patient endurance* you will save your lives" (21:19). Even though "the end" may not come soon, even though the kingdom of God may not be fully established on earth until Jesus comes again in glory, those who carry Jesus' cross of love daily and with patient endurance are saving their lives and really making his kingdom present in the world, *today!*

The Kingdom of God Today

There is a great need for a Lucan spirituality of the present moment in the twentieth century struggle for justice. While the desire to see God's kingdom "established in power" is what motivates Christians to work for social change, the struggle is truly Christian only when passionate *zeal for the kingdom* is accompanied by a deeply grounded, humble *trust in the Lord of the kingdom.* On the one hand, it is painfully obvious that God's kingdom has not yet fully come. Consequently, in a world so full of unrest and injustice, Christians cannot be at rest within themselves. They have to join in the struggle, challenging and critiquing whatever persons or structures that allow the world to be as it is. On the other hand, in the Lucan "now time" of the kingdom, the Lord of justice *is here,* "even in our midst." His Spirit is active as a reconciling force, enlivening his people with passionate courage and relentless hope, even when the monumental task might otherwise lead them to bitter frustration or joyless despair. Thus enlivened, Christian agents of justice recognize that the kingdom is present now, even in little victories and seemingly insignificant steps towards peace. And they rejoice in them, with gratitude. While they continue to lay down their lives for their convictions and for a "more just tomorrow," they are also convinced that such justice will come with "many todays," todays of calm trust versus angry frustration, todays of humble courage versus anxious worry.

The bottom line of God's kingdom, according to Luke, might very well be expressed in one of the eucharistic acclamations of the Catholic liturgy, so rich in meaning: "When we eat this bread and drink this cup (being one with Jesus and his cross, in the present), we proclaim your death, Lord Jesus (acknowledging the saving effects of his death, in the past), until you come in glory (longing for the fullness of his kingdom, in the future)." Indeed, as Luke's readers turn to the next chapter, on eucharist and discipleship, they will be invited to "taste and see how good the Lord is," the Lord of the kingdom! When we eat this bread and drink this cup, may our longing for justice and peace be nourished, until we all eat in the kingdom of God!

2

ON THE EUCHARIST AND CHRISTIAN DISCIPLESHIP

"The liturgy is the source and summit of Christian spirituality." This single, brief statement of the Second Vatican Council captures what might well be the touchstone of the Catholic Church's self-understanding. For Luke also, the eucharist is "of the essence" of being a disciple of Jesus. From what shall soon be discovered in this examination of the eucharist and discipleship in Luke's writings, it might even be accurate to say that Vatican II paraphrased Luke, who describes Jesus at the Last Supper as "the one in our midst who serves us" (22:27). For Luke, the eucharist, *as an act of loving service,* is the source and summit of Christian spirituality! In these pages, Luke's readers will observe Jesus and his disciples as they eat with sinners and outsiders. They will experience the literary genius of Luke once more as he expresses how central Christain service is to Christian eucharist. They will learn how "the breaking of the bread," the Lucan phrase for eucharist in the Acts of the Apostles, is meant to nourish the whole earthly Body of Christ on its journey to the heavenly banquet!

"He Eats with Sinners"

Throughout Luke's gospel, Jesus eats with sinners. His healing ministry has hardly begun when he accepts the invitation of Levi, a tax collector and one of the "first called," to eat in his home (5:27-32). A large crowd of Levi's friends are with him when the Pharisees ask: "Why do you eat and drink with tax collectors and non-observers of the Law?" (v. 30). In response, Jesus calls himself a doctor, who has come for those who need him, not for the healthy (in v. 31). Then, he concludes: "I have come, not to invite the self-righteous to a change of heart, but sinners" (v. 32). Shortly after this, once more in the context of a dinner, this time in the house of a leading Pharisee, Jesus forgives the sinner woman and challenges the "sinless Simon" to follow her example (7:36-52). Such encounters "at meal time" lead to conflicts with those who recognize Jesus' preference for the outcasts. You can tell who a person is by the company he keeps, by the people she eats with! "And this one welcomes sinners and eats with them!" (15:2). This is how Luke begins his memorable chapter on forgiveness, which includes not only the parable of the prodigal sons (vv. 11-32), but also the parables of the lost sheep-sinner (vv. 4-7) and of the lost coin-sinner (vv. 8-10). By placing chapter 15 in the context of "eating with sinners," Luke subtly but unmistakeably makes "welcoming sinners" an essential part of "eating with Jesus."

In the light of Jesus' words and practice, those who believe that they are unworthy to eat with Jesus at eucharist can take heart. "He came for us sinners. He wants to eat with us today! He wants us to join him for dinner!" Such news is almost too good to be true. "Yet, it *is* true," says Luke. Observe Peter, for instance. Here was a disciple of Jesus, who had been close to him from the beginning. He denied him three times at the crucial time of Jesus' trial. He was the greatest of sinners, and he knew it. He wept bitterly (22:62). Nonetheless, even he learned that "eating with sinners" was Jesus' way of drawing people to himself. As a consequence, in the face of reproach from his peers, "he entered the house of the uncircumcised Cornelius and *ate with him*" (Acts 11:3)! Christian pilgrims who hear Luke's good news today will not only be encouraged out of their sense of unworthiness in relating with Jesus, they will also let the eucharistic meal be for others what it was for the primitive church, "the welcoming source and summit of true Christian living."

The Special "Flavor" of Luke's Eucharistic Meal

All the passages that concern meals and eating in Luke's gospel lead up to his version of the Last Supper (in ch. 22). This is especially true in the case of his account of the multiplication of the loaves for over five thousand hungry people at Bethsaida (9:10-17). There is so much "eucharistic language" in this miraculous feeding that it begs for comparison with the supper scene:

> Taking the five loaves and the two fish, Jesus raised his eyes to heaven, pronounced a blessing over them, broke them, and gave them to his disciples for distribution to the crowd. They all

> ate until they had enough. What they had left, over and above, filled twelve baskets. (9:16f.).
>
> Taking bread and giving thanks, he broke it and gave it to them, saying, 'This is my body to be given to you. Do this as a remembrance of me.' (22:19)

It is almost as if Jesus is saying: "Hurry from Bethsaida to the upper room in Jerusalem! There is more than enough for you to eat there!"

All the evangelists seem to draw their readers toward the Christian community meal. They sensed that it was there, in the eucharist, that the risen Lord would come to be experienced and known better than in any other way. However, when one reads the Lucan version of the Last Supper (22:14-30) along side the Marcan and Matthean accounts (Mk 14:22-26 & Mt 26:26-30), one cannot miss Luke's obvious emphasis. The special ingredient which Luke has added to the eucharistic meal is discovered in his expansion of the supper scene to include the dispute about "who should be regarded as the greatest" among the disciples (vv. 24-29).

> He said: 'Earthly kings lord it over their people. Those who exercise authority over them are called their benefactors. Yet it cannot be that way with you. Let the greater among you be as the junior, the leader as the servant. Who, in fact is greater —he who reclines at table or he who serves the meal? Is it not the one who reclines at table? Yet *I am in your midst as the one who serves you.*' (22:25-27).

All of the evangelists record the confusion Jesus caused at the supper when he predicted that his betrayer was present. But only Luke indicates, by his placement of the dispute over "who is the greatest" here, that there are more ways than one to betray him. Indeed, for Luke and his readers, the issue in the early church of "servant leadership versus ambition for authority" overshadows Judas' betrayal. And that vital issue is resolved *at the supper:* "I am in your midst as the one who serves you." Consequently, at every remembrance of Jesus' death, at every eucharist from that point on, Christians would be compelled to recall the heart of it all: "Let the greater among you be as the junior, the leader as the servant." When Luke brings eucharist and humble service together in this way, he makes explicit what Mark and Matthew had said implicitly. Their "suffering servant" passages occurred in the earlier stages of their gospels. James and John, and their mother, posed the "ambition question" on the way to Jerusalem (see Mk 10:35-45 and Mt 20:20-28). It was *before* entering the city that the disciples heard Jesus respond: "The Son of Man has come, not to be served by others, but to serve, to give his own life as a ransom for the many (Mt 20:28 and Mk 10:45). Luke's Jesus says it in Jerusalem, in the upper room, in the course of the meal! The fourth evangelist, John, will follow Luke's lead. He even goes further, when he *replaces* the Last Supper (there are no "eucharistic words" in John's gospel!) with:

> During the supper, Jesus rose from the meal and took off his cloak. He picked up a towel and tied it around himself. Then he poured water into a basin and began to wash his disciples' feet and dry them with the towel he had around him. (Jn 13:3-5).

John's "Last Supper" therefore, like Luke's, is transformed into a final symbolic act of service. "But if I washed your feet — I who am teacher and Lord — then you must wash each other's feet. What I just did was to give you an example: as I have done, so you must do" (Jn 13:14-15). John and Luke thus add a similar, special flavor to the Christian eucharistic meal. Its savor is *service!* And he whom Christians meet, when they approach the "source and summit of spirituality," is "the one who serves."

Coming to Know Jesus in "The Breaking of the Bread"

For Luke, the eucharist means service. This is true, not only in the isolated experience of the first eucharist, but also during the time of Jesus' post-resurrection appearances through to the end of the Acts of the Apostles. The members of the early church, and all members of the church who travel on *Journey D* with Luke, *live out* this special form of eucharistic spirituality whenever they nourish the living body of Christ, whenever they serve others as did Jesus, the "suffering servant." In the earlier chapters of this book, Luke's readers have come to know Jesus as a compassionate healer and as a courageous preacher of peace, generosity, and forgiveness. As "the one who serves," Jesus fed his people his own body and blood on the night before he died. His death on the cross the next day proved that he meant what he said. It was as a suffering servant and "lover of his people unto death" that Jesus wanted to be remembered: "Do this in memory of me" (22:19).

But how soon they forget! With all this intimate experience of Jesus behind them, the disciples were at a complete loss after Jesus' death. Even after the news of the women that he had been raised from the dead, Luke reports that *only* Peter ran to the tomb to see (24:9-12). The others "refused to believe them, for the women's story seemed like nonsense to them" (v. 11). They needed "the reminder," says Luke. They needed the eucharist! And so, "as two of them were making their way to a village named Emmaus . . ." (24:13ff.). The dramatic encounter of the disciples with Jesus on the way to Emmaus is forever etched in the Christian memory. By means of the account, Luke not only emphasizes that Jesus is "among the living" but also that he can truly be known only in the experience of "the breaking of the bread" and *all that it signifies!* Indeed, the hearts of the two disciples "burned inside them as he talked to them on the road and explained the Scriptures to them (v. 32). But it was only when he had "seated himself with them to eat, had taken the bread, pronounced the blessing, had broken the bread and begun to distribute it to them, that their eyes were opened and they recognized him" (vv. 30-31). It was "in the breaking of the bread that they had come to know him" (v. 35). It was in this eucharist on the road to Emmaus that they remembered! He would be known forever *in the meal,* in "the breaking of the bread."

Becoming Christ, the Servant, in Eucharist

Regarding the body of Christ, St. Augustine said: "We become what we eat." If he was right, the church that *comes to know* Jesus in the breaking of the bread *becomes* the servant church when it eats his body. In the early chapters of the Acts, Luke presents his pilgrim church with an ideal picture of the early church becoming Christ. They broke the bread for others! "They devoted themselves to the apostles' instructions and the communal life, to the breaking of the bread and the prayers . . . Those who believed shared all things in common;

they would sell their property and goods, dividing everything among them on the basis of each one's needs" (Acts 2:42 & 44f.). The early church became Christ. Their lives proved that they remembered the meaning of the meal and the significance of Jesus' whole life and death. Christian eucharist leads, by necessity, to attention and concrete love for the whole body of Christ: "For all who owned property or homes sold them and donated the proceeds. They laid them at the feet of the apostles to be distributed to everyone according to their need" (Acts 4:34f.) "Taking the five loaves and the two fish, Jesus raised his eyes to heaven, pronounced a blessing over them, broke them, and gave them to his disciples for distribution to the crowd" (Lk 9:16). According to Luke, the Christian eucharist has no meaning, unless those who participate in it "become what they eat" and distribute that life-giving food, Christ himself, to the hungry crowds!

Paul learned the lesson. His communion with Jesus converted him from being persecutor to being nourisher of the Christian community. His letters are food for his brothers and sisters "in Christ." In the Acts, Luke's readers find Paul at eucharist with his faith community in Troas. "On the first day of the week, when we gathered for the breaking of the bread, Paul preached to them" (Acts 20:7). But he preached so long that the young lad, Eutychus, fell asleep and fell from the window to his death (v. 9). It seems that Luke preserved this story for the sake of what follows. After Paul rushes downstairs, draws the boy to himself, and assures the alarmed people "there is life in him" (v. 10), "he went upstairs again, broke bread and ate" (v. 11)! Can Luke be suggesting that there will be times in life when even "the breaking of the bread" does not seem to "give life" to people? And even so, if there are enough people like Paul around, ready to respond actively, to take up slack, to nurture the life of the Christian community, then the church can say with confidence: "There is life in us! It is the life of Christ, the servant Lord! So let us continue to break the bread and share it with the world!"

There is one final passage in the Acts that concerns the eucharist, or at least a veiled reference to it. Paul has the feature role, once again. This time it is on the high sea (in Acts 27:6-32), when, in the midst of a severe storm, he asks his companions to keep up their courage. His word gave them hope, but it was not until the fourteenth day, when he "took some bread, gave thanks to God before all of them, broke it, and began to eat" that they really "received new courage . . . And they too had something to eat" (vv. 35f.). After several more critical incidents, "all came safely ashore" (v. 44). This account lets Luke's readers know that the fruit of a spirituality rooted in the eucharist is renewed courage in the face of unexpected "storms" on the Christian way. At the same time, the eucharist does not "do it all for you." Paul and his shipmates did all they possibly could do in order to survive. They weighed anchor when gentle winds finally came. They used cables to brace the ship. They threw cargo and gear over the side to avoid sinking. They took soundings so as not to dash against some rocky, underwater crags. They prayed for daylight. In the last analysis, however, *they ate* with Paul. Their renewed courage came from the breaking of the bread. As it was on the treacherous seas off Malta (28:1), so it is on the often turbulent seas of twentieth century life. Yet there is renewed strength and safe harbor for those whose lives are centered on Christ, "in the breaking of the bread."

Summary Note for Ministers of the Eucharist

In the Catholic Church, we are accustomed to call our altar boys and girls "servers." They "serve Mass" and help the priest at the altar. According to Luke, the real "servers" at eucharist are the servant celebrants and preachers, the servant ministers of the word, of communion, of music, and of hospitality. Since Luke's gospel and Acts are so laden with the message that eucharist means service, renewed life, and "eating with the outcasts," the primary Lucan focus for all "servers' of the eucharist is a *welcoming hospitality.*" With all due reverence to the inspired word of God which they proclaim, readers and homilists will show an equal amount of respect for their listeners, especially for those who come to eucharist burdened with a sense of unworthiness and personal sinfulness. At the time of holy communion, those who distribute the Body of Christ will do more than exercise care with the sacred host. They will recognize the face of Christ in the faces of the communicants, their fellow pilgrims and brothers and sisters in the living body of Christ. They will also see, with their "Christian peripheral vision," the many other members of Christ's body who are *not* present, as well as those who *are* present but who still do not feel welcomed to approach the table of the Lord. They will love them too. They will do whatever they can to bring them "home," to *their* table! Finally, the ministers who bring communion to the sick, once the community eucharist has ended, will reverence those they visit as profoundly as the host they carry with them. In a "Lucan spirit" all the "servers" at eucharist will cooperate to make it clear that "this is a community of one heart and of one mind, which respects everyone as equals and wants to draw all people into the one 'servant family' of Jesus Christ."

It is hard work for "the servers" to be so responsive to the needs of the congregation. Sometimes one might find oneself saying, "I wish I could pray at the eucharist myself!" But when service and hospitality are the focus of liturgy planning and experience, Jesus himself is present to nourish the servers as well as "the served." And without falling into the trap of "performing," those who come to know Christ "in the breaking of the bread" will be able to taste what the early church community tasted.

> With exultant and sincere hearts, they will take their meals in common, praising God and winning the approval of all the people. Day by day the Lord will add to their number those who are being saved. (Paraphrase of Acts 2:46f.).

3

JOY: THE FINAL CHAPTER

Intimately connected with eucharist, as well as with most of the Lucan themes treated thus far in this book, is *Christian joy.* Luke knew his human community well. He knew of their hopes and fears. He knew his brothers and sisters as well as he had come to know his Lord, Jesus. Because of being "so in touch" with God and his people Luke would "color the world" with the rich hues of happiness and delight. He did so because of Jesus' saving death and resurrection. He also filled the pages of his gospel and Acts with exultation because of the human tendency toward fear, fear in the face of the marvelous, fear in the experience of being "a new Christian community" in a time of transition (see opening chapter of this book for a sketch of Luke's times). As a consequence, it is not surprising to discover the following "joy vs. fear" pattern, throughout Luke's writings.

Do not be frightened, Zechariah. (1:13)
Do not be afraid, Mary. (1:30)
You have nothing to fear, shepherds. (2:10a)

Do not be afraid, Peter. (5:10a)
Do not live in fear,
little flock (12:32a).

It has pleased your Father to give you the kingdom! (12:32b)
From now on, Peter, you will be catching others (for God)! (5:10b)
Shepherds, I come to proclaim good news to you — *tidings of great joy* to be shared by the whole people! (2:10b)
My being proclaims the greatness of the Lord, *my spirit finds joy* in God my savior! (1:46f.)
Blessed be the Lord the God of Israel, because he has visited and ransomed his people (1:68)

Today's world and church are as much in need of this heartening word of Luke as was the first community of Christians for whom he wrote. In the face of fear, Luke's gospel is the gospel of unbelievable joy! When Elizabeth proclaims "Blest is she who trusted that the Lord's words to her would be fulfilled" (1:45), she is speaking to her cousin Mary, who will bring Jesus into the world. But she is also speaking to all Christians who long for the happiness of the Lord in their inmost beings. When Peter preaches at Pentecost, his first sermon in the Acts sums up all that has been and all that will be as a result of Jesus' life among his people on earth.

> People of Israel, listen to me! Jesus the Nazorean was a man whom God sent to you with miracles, wonders, and signs as his credentials. These God worked through him in your midst, as you well know. He was delivered up by the set purpose and plan of God; you even made use of pagans to crucify and kill him. God freed him from death's bitter pangs, however, and raised him up again, for it was impossible that death should keep its

> hold on him. David says of him: 'I have set the Lord ever before me, with him at my right hand I shall not be disturbed. *My heart has been glad and my tongue has rejoiced,* my body will live on in hope, for you will not abandon my soul to the nether world, nor will you suffer your faithful one to undergo corruption. You have shown me the paths of life; *you will fill me with joy in your presence.'* (Acts 2:22-28).

Peter's first preaching reflects the initial preaching of Jesus. Jesus came "to announce a year of favor from the Lord" (4:19). And after he had rolled up the scroll, he said "Today this scripture passage is fulfilled in your hearing!" (4:21). In this final chapter on Christian joy, Luke's readers are invited to experience the joy of the Lord's year of favor. They will travel one last time through the stages of journey, which Luke has laid out for them. As Christians discover Luke's constant concern for their happiness, which involves all the characters of his infancy story (*Journey* A), of Jesus' own journey (*Journey* B), and of the early church's pilgrimage (*Journey* C), they are certain to "catch the Lucan spirit of joy" on their own stage of the journey. They will realize his overriding concern that they themselves be a spontaneous, joyful people of God!

The Four Terms

More than sixty references to joy and happiness appear in Luke's two volume work. He uses four different Greek terms to express his message:

> *chairō,* meaning "to rejoice, to be glad, great favor, gracious care";
> *euphrainō,* meaning "to gladden, to cheer, to celebrate, great delight";

> *agalliaō*, meaning "to exult, to be overjoyed, to be full of exultation";
> *makarizō*, meaning "to be blest, to be fortunate, to be full of joy."

While the four terms are clearly synonymous, each one can connote a certain, special "flavor" of joy. Therefore, when two of the synonyms occur together in the same passage, one can notice the nuances which shade Luke's meaning. For example, at the conclusion of Jesus' parable of the forgiving father and his two prodigal sons, Luke has the father say to the older son: "My son, you are with me always, and everything I have is yours. But we had to celebrate (*euphrainō*, festive celebration) and rejoice (*chairō*, feeling the profound joy of it all)! This brother of yours was dead and has come back to life. He was lost and is found" (15:32). Likewise, the angel Gabriel "bombards" Zechariah with the promise that joy (*chara*) and gladness (*agaliasis*, exultation in the hope of the coming Messiah) will be his at the birth of his son, John (1:14). In the visitation scene, the baby, John, leapt in Elizabeth's womb for joy (with more of the messianic expectation of *agalliasis*) at Mary's arrival. But "blest are you among women" (the state of being greatly favored by God, *makaria*) cries out Elizabeth. And shortly after this, Mary herself takes up both terms and prays: "My spirit finds joy (*agalliaō*) in God my savior, for he has looked upon his servant in her lowliness; all ages to come shall call me blessed (*makarizō*). While the four terms for joy can be used interchangeably at times, it is interesting and sometimes enlightening for Luke's readers to examine the special force which the various Greek terms bear within them.

Joy to the World

Predominant among the four words Luke uses to express joy is *chairō.* This is the term commonly used in the New Testament for "grace, favor, and the profound joy of God," bestowed in Jesus. Luke's use of the term follows the lead of his contemporaries. But he also expresses, explicitly, that this joyful favor is meant to be shared by the *whole* world! *Many* will rejoice in the birth of John (1:14). *All* of Elizabeth's neighbors rejoiced with her upon hearing the news "that God had extended his mercy to her" (1:58). The news of Jesus' birth is not only for the shepherds, but is to be shared "with the whole people!" (2:10). The joy Christians know in Jesus' becoming like them is not to be "treasured in one's heart." It is meant to be shared! This Lucan concern for "communal joy" continues in *Journey B,* the story of Jesus. Shortly after the badly stooped woman was cured, "his opponents were covered with confusion; meanwhile, *everyone else rejoiced* at the marvels Jesus was accomplishing" (13:17). Later, as Jesus entered Jerusalem, "*the entire crowd* of disciples began to rejoice and praise God loudly for the display of power they had seen!" (19:37). "*Everyone,*" says Luke, "must be overjoyed in Jesus' presence among them, in Jesus' healing, saving power!"

An even richer understanding of this first term for joy emerges when Luke's readers learn how closely it is related to *forgiveness,* in chapter 15. "There will be *more joy in heaven over one repentant sinner* than over ninety-nine righteous people who have no need to repent" (15:7 & 10). The shepherd who had lost his single sheep called all his neighbors to rejoice with him when he found it. The woman who had lost her silver piece likewise called in all her friends, saying; "Rejoice with me! I have found the silver piece I lost!"

Another Lucan "joy connection" helps Christians to carry on their mission of preaching God's word, especially in the face of the discouragement and *suffering* that such a mission often entails. As Jesus' disciples begin their mission, Jesus encourages them: "On the day when they insult you and hate you, *rejoice* and exult, for your reward shall be great in heaven. Thus it was that their fathers treated the prophets" (6:23). As Jesus leaves them for his heavenly home, he promises them the promise of his Father (the Holy Spirit), which will enable them to preach "penance for the remission of sins to all the nations" (24:47 & 49). They, in turn, "fell down to do him reverence, and then returned to Jerusalem *filled with joy!*" (v. 52). The gospel of Luke begins and ends with rejoicing. *Journey A* and *B* are journeys of joy. And so is *Journey C!*

The joy of Jesus' birth and resurrection flows into the mainstream of the early church's life in the Acts of the Apostles. The continuing mission and preaching of the first disciples bring with them the same "connections" as were present in Jesus' life. In Acts 5:32, the Sanhedrin were stunned to fury and wanted to kill Peter and the other disciples for preaching God's word. However, in Acts 5:41, Luke reports that "the disciples, for their part, left the Sanhedrin *full of joy* that they had been judged worthy of ill treatment for the sake of the Name (Jesus). Day after day, both in the temple and at home, they never stopped teaching and proclaiming the good news of Jesus, the Messiah." After the murder of Stephen, the members of the church who had been dispersed went about preaching the word. Philip, for example, went down to the town of Samaria and there proclaimed the Messiah.

> Without exception, the crowds that heard Philip and saw the miracles he performed attended closely to what he had to say. There were many who had unclean spirits, which came out shrieking loudly. Many others were paralytic and cripples, and these were cured. *The rejoicing in that town rose to fever pitch.* (Acts 8:1-8).

Everywhere the apostles preached, the same thing happened. "The Gentiles *were delighted* when they heard the word and responded with praise. All who were destined for life everlasting believed in it" (Acts 13:48). And although the Jews finally expelled them from their territory, "the disciples could not but be *filled with joy* in the Holy Spirit" (13:52). Joy was the result of preaching. Conversion from sin was the result of joyful preaching. And all the suffering that came along with it was endurable, indeed, was *to be rejoiced in,* because the Spirit of the risen Jesus was vibrantly alive in the early church.

Such joy, as is expressed by *chairo,* is exposed for "what it is not" and for "what it really is." It is not the "Polyanna" type of giddiness, often associated with people who live "on the surface of things." It is not the "I love you, Jesus, and you love me, and make me happy" sort of shallow joy that comes and goes so easily. Lucan joy is a profound gladness that is rooted in the person of Jesus, in the word of God, and in the reality of the earthly, daily growth *and suffering,* which make up the Christian journey of faith. It "comes with the territory." Christian joy enables pilgrims to be missionaries, bringing the good news of God's forgiveness and favor to the whole world!

Of Feasting and Parties

Luke is the only evangelist to use the Greek verb *euphraino,* expressing "gladness, celebration, delight, feasting" (6 times in the gospel, 4 times in the Acts). The key to the special meaning of this word for joy is revealed by Luke's first usage of it. In the parable of the rich man, who chose to sit back with all his grain and goods, the "earthly" side of joy emerges: "You have blessings in reserve for years to come. Relax! Eat heartily, drink well. *Enjoy yourself!*" (12:19). Another rich man, Lazarus, who dressed in purple and linen, "*feasted splendidly* every day" (16:19). Both of them would get their "just desserts" for their self-indulgent pleasure. But this same term, connoting an earthy, fulfilling, pleasureable experience, is also found to be appropriate by Luke to describe the banquet which God has prepared for those who return to him from their sinful ways. One can almost feel the hearty "gusto" of a "real life party" as the forgiving father prepares for the return of his younger son. "Let us eat and *celebrate!*" (15:23). This joy is not a state of mind. It is not a quiet, meditative mood of tranquility. No! Instead, the fatted calf is butchered for the feast. There is raucous music and dancing here, which attracts party-goers and disturbs the resentful, older son (15:25f.). The relationship of a son and his father has been restored. There is reason for a "full-blown party" here! God and his children are one again in Christ and in reconciliation. Let us celebrate! Let us party, and let us do so splendidly!!

In the Acts of the Apostles, one finds more of the same. Luke tries to make it clear that God wants his church-in-time to enjoy their union with him, with abandon! The first two references to this kind of joy in the Acts occur in Peter's Pentecost speech. Quoting David, he says:

> My heart *has been glad* and my tongue has rejoiced . . . You will not abandon my soul to the nether world, nor will you allow your faithful one to undergo corruption. You have shown me the path to life; you will *fill me with joy* (festive delight) in your presence. (Acts 2:26-28).

Such delight comes to Peter and to all his hearers because of God's love for his people, bringing Jesus, "his faithful one," to life. Just as Peter invited those gathered at Pentecost to enjoy and taste the presence of God's life, so also Luke invites all Christians living in the age of the Spirit *to enjoy life, to the fullest!*

The final two mentions of this euphoric joy assure Luke's readers that he means what he says. In Acts 7:41, Stephen describes how God "turned away from his people and abandoned them to the worship of the galaxies of the heavens," because they "fashioned the golden calf, offered sacrifice to the idol, and *had a festive celebration* over the product of their own hands." Theirs was a wild party worthy of condemnation. Yet, it is the same God, says Luke, who loves the creation of his hands so much that:

> In past ages he let the Gentiles go their way. Yet in bestowing his benefits, he has not hidden himself completely, without a clue. From the heavens he sends down rain and rich harvest; your spirits he fills with food and *delight (euphrosynes).* (Acts 14:17).

What wonderful news for God's people of every race, of every age! What is very earthy and very harmful (self-indulgence in one's own creation) can be very earthy and very good, when it is of God. The living God *delights* in all he created! And he wants his most precious creation, his people, *to indulge* in the rest of creation with him! "Quick! Bring out the finest robe and put it on them. Put rings on their fingers and shoes on their feet. Take the fatted calf and kill it. Let us eat and celebrate because this people of mine was dead and has come back to full life. They have been wandering, lost, but I have found them!" (paraphrase of Luke 15:22-24). And may the party go on!

This Is It! Messianic Exultation

In the time of Jesus' life and the early church, the whole Jewish people was eagerly expecting the coming of the Messiah, the one who would deliver them from evil and bring them to the heavenly banquet with God. The Christian faith community, of course, believed that Jesus was the promised Messiah. He had already come. He had already delivered his people. He had already gone to prepare a place for them at the heavenly table. The Christian "waiting for the day" was, therefore, filled with an *exultant* and sure hope. Luke's third term for joy, *agalliao,* captures that exuberant hope. "They went to the temple area together every day; while in their homes they broke bread. With *exultant* and sincere hearts they took their meals in common, praising God and winning the approval of all the people" (Acts 2:46f.). But theirs was not an escapist "dream hope" for instant heavenly bliss. Rather, says Luke, the first Christians lived out their messianic joy in the present reality of their lives. In the power of the Holy Spirit they shared their lives, their goods, and their joy with each other (Acts 4:32-35).

The story of Paul and the jailer at Philippi (Acts 16:25-34), dramatically brings out how Christians already have a foretaste of the messianic joy that will one day be theirs in fullness.

> About midnight, while Paul and Silas were praying and singing hymns to God as their fellow prisoners listened, a severe earthquake suddenly shook the place, rocking the prison to its foundation. Immediately, all the doors flew open and everyone's chains were pulled loose. The jailer woke up to see the prison gates wide open. Thinking that the prisoners had escaped, he drew his sword to kill himself, but Paul shouted to him: "Do not harm yourself! We are still here.' (vv. 25-28).

After the jailer had asked for a share in what was obviously "of God" they preached God's word to him and to everyone of his household. And what happened next? "He and his whole household were baptized. And he led them up to his house, spread a table before them, and *joyfully celebrated* with his whole family his new found faith in God" (vv. 33-34).

In such prayerful, joyful meals and celebrations, Luke says that the church realistically appropriated the joy of the Messiah's victory. They shared their lives, their faith, and their confidence with others, both believers and non-believers. All came to experience what Zechariah, Elizabeth, and Mary had experienced, by anticipation, before them.

> Joy and (messianic) *gladness* will be yours, and many will rejoice in John's birth! (1:14).
> The baby in my womb *leapt for joy* at your greeting. (1:44).
> My spirit *exults* in God my savior! (1:47).

Yes, says Luke, the whole family of God can rejoice (*agalliao*) in the Holy Spirit because "what the Father of heaven and earth has hidden from the learned and the clever, he has revealed to the merest children" (10:21). How blest are we, children of the kingdom!

How Blest Are We!

The fourth and "final word" for Lucan joy is *makarizo.* Both Luke and Matthew choose this term to express the "happiness of the poor, the hungry, the weeping, etc." in Jesus' beatitudes (Mt 5:3-11 & Lk 6:20f.). Luke also has Mary praise God for the "heaps of happiness" that are hers, for which "all generations shall call her blest!" (1:48). While Mark never once mentions this kind of "blessedness" and John does so only twice (Jn 13:17 & 20:29), Luke develops it into a theme of "God's favor" that pervades his whole gospel. There are three instances that best bring Luke's readers to the source of what "being favored by God" is all about. It is with the examination of these three passages that this "final chapter" concerning Lucan spirituality comes to a close.

1. "*Blessed are they* who hear the word of God and keep it" (11:29). The source of Christian happiness is openness to God, an attentive ear to his word. The poor are promised this reward of blessedness. Mary experienced it (1:46-47) and responded faithfully, with her whole life. Christians who hear God's word and keep it will respond concretely to the needs of their brothers and sisters, other beloved children of God, with a Lucan spirit of prayer, compassion, and generosity. Such "heaps of happiness" as Mary knew are meant for all who "keep God's word."

2. "*How blessed will those servants be* whom the master finds wide awake upon his return. I tell you, he will put on an

apron, seat them at table, and proceed to wait on them. Should he happen to come at midnight, or before sunrise, and find them prepared, how happy shall they be!" (12:37f.). Servants and handmaidens of the Lord, alert to the spirit of justice and peace that Luke's writings proclaim, will challenge the world, full of hopelessness and oppression, with a festive and realistic Christian service. It has pleased the Father to give them the kingdom and to build it up. How happy are those who proclaim the year of favor from the Lord and do justice!

3. "*Happy is the one* who eats bread in the kingdom of God" (14:15). The kingdom of God has been established here on earth with the life, death, and resurrection of Jesus. The Spirit of God leads Christian sojourners on towards their sure hope, nourishing them by word and eucharist and courage for their pilgrimage. But the kingdom of God in its fullness is not yet. There is a fullness of joy that still awaits his hungry people, at the end of the journey. Anyone who has traveled prayerfully with Luke through the pages of his gospel and Acts cannot have escaped the passionate love that the Father and Jesus have for those who long for them. May God's people continue to rush to the Fathers's embrace. Let all peoples know Jesus "in the breaking of the bread." And "let us love God (and each other) by the work of our hands and the sweat of our brows" (Vincent de Paul), until all of God's children eat his bread in the kingdom!

WHERE CREDIT IS DUE...

Besides an author's personal love and knowledge of biblical writings, one naturally feels strongly that the acknowledgement of certain other experts in the field is only right and just. Consequently, I list here some few of the books and tools that have helped form me and the fruit of my labors, namely, this work on Luke-Acts. I also hope that the brief remarks about the following works will facilitate my readers in their further study and appreciation of St. Luke's message and meaning for them.

Four books immediately come to mind as having greatly influenced me in my study and preparation of this volume. First, Charles Talbert's *Literary Patterns, Theological Themes and the Genre of Luke-Acts* (Scholars Press, 1974) has long stimulated me to discover and appreciate the inner relationships of various structures and patterns in Luke's writings. The conclusions that one can come to, once such patterns are seen, are powerful indeed. (See how some of these insights come together in my Part Four: Luke As A Literary Genius.) A second book that deals insightfully with the literary contrasts and comparisons among various passages in Luke's gospel is

Helmut Flender's *St. Luke: Theologian of Redemptive History* (Fortress, 1967). Flender's exposition of the various kinds of contrasts and comparisons employed by Luke was very helpful to me, for example, in Part Three: Lucan Themes For The Journey, Of Women and Men. John Navone's *Themes of St. Luke* (Gregorian U. Press, 1970) is another basic treatment of Lucan themes which has helped me and many others come to a richer appreciation of the mind and artistry of Luke. The fourth book I choose to mention here is the classic work by Hans Conzelmann, *The Theology of Saint Luke* (Faber and Faber, 1960), which is the challenging and groundbreaking study of the "journey structure" of Luke's gospel. While there have been many adaptations and correctives to Conzelmann's seminal work, he will always be considered the "father" of Lucan structure criticism. It is worth the time and effort any serious student of Luke will put into reading it.

In scholarly work, one also depends on special works to search out details and particular areas of interest. Of the many such references used in the present work, I single out only three, hoping that my readers will find them useful and in so doing will be led to discover the richness of resources available to students of God's word.

Biblical *periodical literature* is digested and summarized in the wonderful tool known as *New Testament Abstracts* (available from the Catholic Biblical Association). In any given volume one can find articles of interest that help one delve more into special topics. An example of this was my discovery of the article "Good News of Peace," by John Donahue, in *The Way* magazine for April, 1982. Having *New Testament Abstracts* and articles like Donahue's available for my use gave me much confidence as I tried to develop the section of this volume Of Justice And Peace, in Part Three.

Concordances of the Bible are extremely valuable when one is attempting to line up what images or phrases any biblical author uses throughout the various writings in the Bible. I used Michael Darton's *Modern Concordance to the New Testament* in this work, but have also found Nelson's *Complete Concordance of the New American Bible* to be very helpful.

A final biblical tool I wish to mention is *the synopsis.* Since the beginning of critical reflection and analysis of gospel texts, it has proven to be invaluable for scholars to have for their use an organized "side by side" arrangement of similar passages from the four gospels. By having them so lined up in front of one's eyes, it is possible to see the clear differences that each gospel author presents for his readers. This enables the student of the text to grasp the emphasis which each author wishes to bring out of each gospel story. The Synopsis of the Four Gospels (available in Greek-English or English Only editions) by Kurt Aland (United Bible Societies, 1982) seems to be an easy and up-to-date work for those interested in pursuing this aspect of biblical study.

There are many more books and biblical tools that are too many to be mentioned here. But where credit is due, credit is given. And I hope this simple listing of some of the rich resources of biblical writings enables my readers to go farther along on the journey with the word, if they so desire.

OLD TESTAMENT INDEX

NEW TESTAMENT INDEX

Romans

1 Corinthians

Galatians

Ephesians

1 Thessalonians